Painted Travels

Painted Travels

SJ AXELBY

PAVILION

For Mummy

Pavilion
An imprint of HarperCollins*Publishers* Ltd
1 London Bridge Street
London SE1 9GF

www.harpercollins.co.uk

HarperCollins*Publishers*
Macken House, 39/40 Mayor Street Upper
Dublin 1, D01 C9W8, Ireland

10 9 8 7 6 5 4 3 2 1

First published in Great Britain by
Pavilion, an imprint of HarperCollins*Publishers* Ltd 2023

Copyright © SJ Axelby 2023

SJ Axelby asserts the moral right to be identified as the
author of this work. A catalogue record for this book is
available from the British Library.

ISBN 978-0-00-858072-8

Publishing Director Stephanie Milner
Managing Editor Clare Double
Editorial Assistant Shamar Gunning
Design Director Laura Russell
Design Assistant Lily Wilson
Layout design Hannah Naughton
Illustrations SJ Axelby
Senior Production Controller Grace O'Byrne

Scanning by Amersham Business Services
Reproduction by Rival
Printed and bound by Rotolito S.p.A.

Cover: Hotel Cipriani, a Belmond hotel, Venice (Belmond/
Marco Valmarana)

MIX
Paper | Supporting
responsible forestry
FSC™ C007454
www.fsc.org

This book is produced from independently certified FSC™
paper to ensure responsible forest management.

For more information visit:
www.harpercollins.co.uk/green

Contents

Foreword by Martina Mondadori

I first chanced upon SJ's work in lockdown when she painted Peter Copping's Normandy home for Christie's Auction House. The photoshoot could not take place due to the restrictions at the time and so they asked if she could superimpose the antiques into his home via her watercolour interior portraiture. She not only captured the light but there was a timelessness about her work and painting style. A few weeks later, my friend Idarica Gazzoni (@arjumands_world) made me aware of @roomportaitclub. SJ set this up as a weekly challenge where she chose a room, posted it on Instagram and people around the world interpret it in any medium they liked, from paint to pastel; embroidery to pen and ink. I was thrilled she has used a couple of images from *Cabana* magazine that had resulted in over 200 different takes on the same spaces.

I have always loved interior portraiture because it automatically layers the details of a room giving it a certain atmosphere and instinctive cosiness, and we regularly feature these in *Cabana*. Somehow a painting allows you to envisage a room through the artist's eye, as well as your own, offering a whole new dimension to the image and experience. I was delighted to be included in her first book where she painted my Milan home capturing the textures and feel of the space.

We also collaborated with a series of paintings for *Cabana*, where we carefully selected rooms that featured in the magazine, which SJ translated artfully in paint and we even had special portfolios made for each one creating a treasured gift.

We share a mutual passion for travel and interiors. The idea of combining travel and painting is certainly not new concept and before the invention of photography it was the way to document such a trip. It is wonderful to see how she documents in paint the interior details and elements that make each of the destinations included in this book such a treat.

Travel *per se* is escapism. *Cabana* is about interiors and travel both as forms of escapism and I am definitely transported by every single one of SJ's travel watercolour portraits. This second book feels like the natural successor to her interior portrait edition.

I have explored many of the interiors featured here myself, from Charleston to the Pitt Rivers Museum in Oxford (my favourite in the world), and it is mind-blowing to see how SJ has captured the atmosphere of these remarkable places.

Whether you are new to SJ's work or a devotee, I am sure you'll embark on a journey with her flicking through every single page of this book.

Bon Voyage!

Introduction

With the exception of painting there is nothing more I love to do than travel and so when the idea came together for a book that combined the two I jumped at the chance. In these pages, I will take you along on a painted tour of remarkable places around the world. Some I have visited in person, others I have only explored in paint, but in each I have aimed to capture the soul of the space.

There are three things I believe make a great visit, it needs to be authentic, it needs to have charm and lastly it needs to leave you with a warm feeling of contentment.

Each place featured here has all three and its own story to tell, with an abundance of character that cannot be replicated. There are some exquisitely grand venues and there are also the homely off-grid sort to explore. This book is a collection of some of my favourite hotels, bars, museums, shops and even a pub. Each is handpicked and has been an utter delight and privilege to paint.

The décor and details will play a huge part in the joy of a venue and each one here has something that makes my heart sing. From the toasty Square and Compass pub in Dorset with its own little museum to the iconic British Pullman train that takes you on a journey back in time. Every single one is a precious experience because of the attention and care the owners or custodians put in and the result is that the visitors get this love out in return.

I find when exploring somewhere in paint, you are forced to focus on details more clearly. I hope to have shared just a few of these with you here and that you enjoy exploring them, too.

Welcome to my painted travels, let the journey begin.

The Destinations

Plan your own painted travels: pick your destination and turn to the page number listed below.

Chatsworth House

Chatsworth – one of the UK's most famous and lavish country houses, located in the Peak District and home to the Duke and Duchess of Devonshire – has always been a centre for creativity and a spot I love to visit. Sixteen generations of the Cavendish family have added to its treasures and, importantly, have moved with the times while restoring and preserving the past. Chatsworth is at its most special at Christmas and the decorations are on another level. We often go up to visit family and enjoy the nearby village of Bakewell at that time of year, and we pop in to Chatsworth when we can. I've never seen so many Christmas trees and the view from the top of the stairs looking down at the baroque Painted Hall is simply stunning. There is even very realistic fake snow gently drifting past the windows out in the Elizabethan courtyard. Each festive season brings a new theme, from Wind in the Willows and Nordic midwinter celebrations to Charles Dickens, and even the biggest Scrooge will find it hard to not feel the warmth of Christmas here.

One of my favourite rooms is the library, featured here. Despite boasting an impressive collection of real books, it is the 'invisible library' that makes it noteworthy. In 1831, the 6th Duke of Devonshire commissioned a set of fake book spines, each with its own amusing fabricated title, some suggested by the Duke's friends. They look like the real deal, first editions of beautiful old books but with titles such as *Knick Knacks* by Paddy Whack and *Sideways through Derbyshire* by Crabbe, which always make me chuckle. The fake books are housed in special bookcases concealing doors that open to stone staircases leading up to the gallery above.

leather band books with brilliantly made-up titles

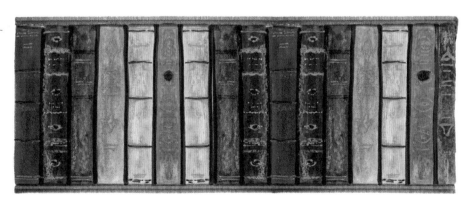

The bedrooms at Chatsworth do not disappoint, and interior lovers will drool over the dreamy chinoiserie wallpapers, shown here in the Regency-style Wellington bedroom. This room was named after the Duke of Wellington, who stayed at Chatsworth in the winter of 1843 during a visit to the house by Queen Victoria. I love the bedroom's serene green tones and the decorative tassels and trimmings on the bed, which, as you can imagine, were extremely tricky to capture in paint.

The gardens that we see today are a must-explore. From the yew maze to the impressive arboretum and grotto, even on a damp Derbyshire day there is joy to be found here. Every aspect of the gardens has been considered, for example the Canal Pond dug in the early 1700s is set a few inches higher than the South Lawn, so that when the house is viewed from the south end of the pond it appears to rise majestically from the water.

I loved having a wander around the sweetest of cottage gardens and the rose garden, designed and planted in 1939 at the request of Mary, wife of the 10th Duke, is worth a look. Many of the original varieties remain including 'Buff Beauty' and my favourite, 'Felicia'.

In the baking hot summer weather of 2022, one layer of the garden's history was revealed. Drone footage showed clearly defined patterns of where the original beds and pathways would have been. The 17th-century parterre, now covered in grass, was exposed for the first time in 300 years. There is so much to discover at Chatsworth – and don't forget to visit the farm shop for some treats to take home.

chinoiserie wallpapers everywhere

Chatsworth maze is well worth exploring - don't get lost though!

tassells & trim galore

San Domenico

This is the Sicilian hotel, adored worldwide, which featured in the second series of the hit TV drama 'White Lotus'. Much like the show, this Taormina hotel is steeped in history and intrigue. For more than 150 years, aristocrats and celebrities have come to take in the breathtaking views of the Ionian Sea and Mount Etna. Guests have included D. H. Lawrence, Oscar Wilde, Sophia Loren and Audrey Hepburn, to name just a few.

A former convent built in the 14th Century, now the monks' cells have been resurrected as hotel bedrooms. Stay here, explore the citrus groves and take in the incredible vistas – it really is as fabulous as it looks on screen. The bedrooms are just the same, too, with the infamous interconnecting doors, plunge pools and paintings of saints made by the monks who once lived here still adorning the walls.

'iconic head vases'

Wander around the hotel and you will spot the ceramic heads that became a symbol of the TV show. These are Sicilian 'teste di moro' and they tell a gruesome tale. The legend goes that in the 11th Century a Moorish man had his head chopped off by his lover after she found out that he was married and about to return to his wife. She made his head into a vase, placed it on her balcony for all to see and grew herbs in it. The heads represent the secrets that can exist between couples and their potential repercussions – and some Sicilian balconies today display a 'testa di moro' as a symbolic reminder to all husbands to behave!

'alfresco dining spot featured in the show

ice cream is served in the sunshine from a charming cart

Cap Rocat

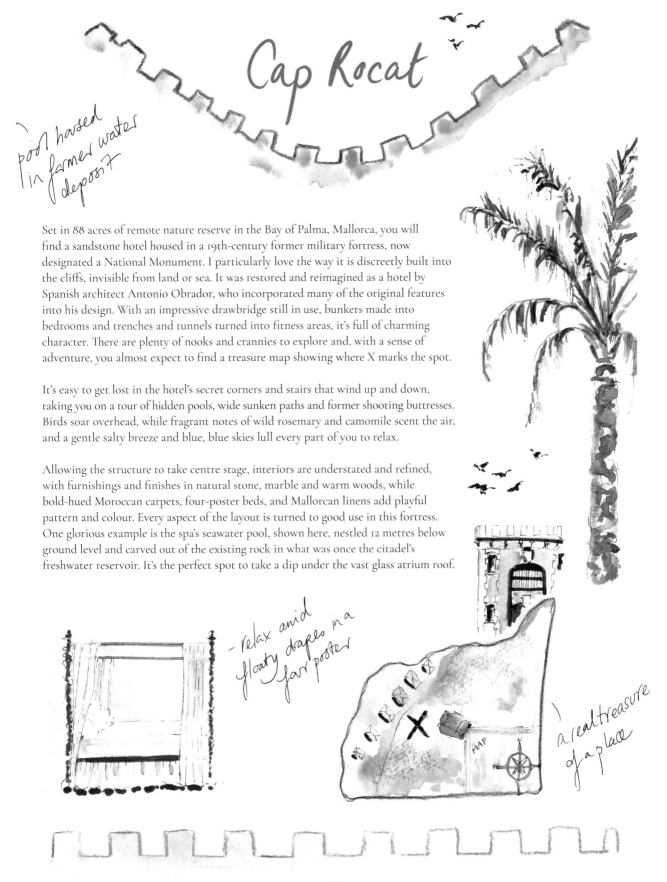

pool housed in former water deposit?

Set in 88 acres of remote nature reserve in the Bay of Palma, Mallorca, you will find a sandstone hotel housed in a 19th-century former military fortress, now designated a National Monument. I particularly love the way it is discreetly built into the cliffs, invisible from land or sea. It was restored and reimagined as a hotel by Spanish architect Antonio Obrador, who incorporated many of the original features into his design. With an impressive drawbridge still in use, bunkers made into bedrooms and trenches and tunnels turned into fitness areas, it's full of charming character. There are plenty of nooks and crannies to explore and, with a sense of adventure, you almost expect to find a treasure map showing where X marks the spot.

It's easy to get lost in the hotel's secret corners and stairs that wind up and down, taking you on a tour of hidden pools, wide sunken paths and former shooting buttresses. Birds soar overhead, while fragrant notes of wild rosemary and camomile scent the air, and a gentle salty breeze and blue, blue skies lull every part of you to relax.

Allowing the structure to take centre stage, interiors are understated and refined, with furnishings and finishes in natural stone, marble and warm woods, while bold-hued Moroccan carpets, four-poster beds, and Mallorcan linens add playful pattern and colour. Every aspect of the layout is turned to good use in this fortress. One glorious example is the spa's seawater pool, shown here, nestled 12 metres below ground level and carved out of the existing rock in what was once the citadel's freshwater reservoir. It's the perfect spot to take a dip under the vast glass atrium roof.

- relax amid floaty drapes in a four poster

a real treasure of a place

Populart

) earthenware vase

Tucked away in the characterful narrow streets of Seville's historic Santa Cruz district is Populart, the most divine shop for antique and modern ceramics. The blue façade against the powerful yellow exterior lures you in and, if you love traditional pottery, from lebrillo bowls to azulejo tiles, this is the place to look for them. I first found this shop while staying at Hacienda de San Rafael (page 122), when I took a day trip to Seville in desperate search of a lebrillo bowl or two to carry home in my hand luggage. I had fallen in love with the way Veere Grenney, one of my favourite interior designers, used these giant Andalusian olive bowls as a novel wall display, and was on the hunt to find my own. I met the lovely Leonardo, who shared stories of the top interior designers that he works with: this is where everyone comes for the authentic stuff. Set up by Laura Salcines in 1977, this shop is almost like a museum, with shelf upon shelf of vases, plates and bowls in every shape and size imaginable. There are tiles, too, in exquisite traditional Spanish designs, from those made by artisans working today to the oldest, most precious objects I would not dare to try to carry home.

) skyblue façade

The earthenware lebrillo bowls with their milky glaze and green flower and leaf motifs simply made my heart sing. Huge, beautiful objects, some the size of a table, that I was definitely going to struggle to get home! After much deliberation and chatting along the way I settled on an 18th-century fajalauza bowl in blue and white. Heavily restored, with metal braces adding character, the bowl made it home in one piece and now sits happily in my kitchen.

~ divine lebrillo bowls

25hours Hotel Indre By

This 19th-century find, located in coolest Copenhagen, is a brilliant design collaboration between 25hours and the Martin Brudnizki Design Studio. In Danish, 'indre by' means 'inner city' and that is exactly where this hotel can be found, smack bang in the city centre. 25hours hotels are dotted across Europe and each has a distinct identity moulded to its location and building, with its own story to tell. The blue awning at the entrance here in Copenhagen displays the motto 'We will never grow up' which certainly sets the tone for what you will find inside.

Coming of Age was the initial concept for 25hours Hotel Indre By, speaking to its heritage as a former porcelain factory and university building. It is a playful, colourful space linking knowledge (a nod to a previous life) and art, which can be enjoyed throughout the hotel.

This is not your usual Scandi hotel; there is an energy and vibrancy here that has been well received by travellers and locals alike. There is a labyrinth of colourful rooms to explore, from the Vinyl Room taking you back to the LPs of your youth to the Love Library and the Boilerman Bar with cocktails aplenty. Bespoke interior details, such as the Pierre Frey curtain fabric designed especially for the hotel, along with Thonet chairs and pieces by Danish makers and artists, make this a very special place to stay. There are two types of bedroom on offer, with a theme of 'passion' or 'knowledge'. Each packs a punch with colour and geometric tiling, and some even have access to a secret garden.

In its former days as a university the Assembly Bar, featured here, is where lecturers and students gathered, and this continues to be the case for guests today. I can't think of a nicer spot to meet up for a coffee.

let's spend the night together

~ the softest pillows

~ enjoy a cycle around the city

playful bedrooms

Alchemist

In the heart of Copenhagen's industrial district is the restaurant Alchemist, a mystical, sensory adventure combining innovative food and exceptional service. The site has an interesting history; it was originally a shipyard's welding hall and after that the Danish Royal Theatre used the space to build their backdrops and sets. The drama lives on today, starting at the grand entrance with imposing doors that lead you into the magnificent dining area, where images are projected onto a gigantic observatory-like domed ceiling. Imagine dining under the dancing waves of light of the *aurora borealis*, under an azure sky of fluttering butterflies, or even an ocean of jellyfish swimming amid plastic rubbish. This is a truly immersive and intriguing experience.

There are high stools to perch on and sociable long tables that wind and twist their way around the space. A typical evening here lasts up to six hours and is divided into various stages, taking you through 50 edible and non-edible 'impressions', with carefully curated wine pairings, too. Every sense is tempted and teased as the staff guide you on this special journey. All they ask of you is to be open to every bit of it.

Jellyfish surprise and delight

hints of the natural world are projected onto the ceiling

alchemy symbols

Alchemist is the brainchild of head chef Rasmus Munk. Championing 'holistic cuisine', which is thought provoking and both humorous and serious, his aim is to reinvent the dining experience in a more meaningful way, and that he definitely does with full marks. He advocates sustainability, health and wellbeing and plans to lead the way in developing awareness in the next generation of chefs and diners alike. Munk even has his own manifesto, stating his vision to 'change the world through gastronomy'. This is more than a restaurant, it's a marvel!

Hauser & Wirth

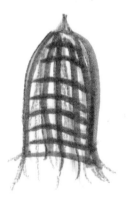

'lobster pot lights hang from the trees

Every year we are lucky enough to holiday in Menorca, our favourite of the Spanish islands for its quieter, laid-back vibe. A pleasant, short boat ride from the capital Mahón takes you to Illa del Rei, a beautiful island where the Hauser & Wirth gallery is located. I first visited in August 2021, when it had only been open for a month. This little island is steeped in history. It is known as 'hospital island' for the former naval hospital constructed here in 1711 by the British, who controlled Menorca for most of the 18th Century. The hospital was abandoned in the 1960s, and in the 1970s it was given heritage protection. It has been very well restored and is a fascinating place to wander around, peer through the windows at the old treatment rooms and wonder what it would have been like to be here as a patient. The beds retain their 1960s mattresses with chamberpots underneath, and the metal medical equipment can still be seen – it's incredibly well preserved. The gallery with its grounds on the same site is a magical place to visit; designed by architect Luis Laplace and landscape designer Piet Oudolf, it is a work of art in itself. The gallery space includes indoor and outdoor installations and an art trail; I was lucky enough to encounter Louise Bourgeois's Spider on the central patio.

The outdoors is as important here as what goes on in the gallery inside. There are plenty of spots for refreshments and lounging. Pinky-beige stones and reclaimed wood are paired with other natural materials to give a relaxed and rustic feel. Lobster pots woven in straw hanging from the trees and blue-and-white striped awnings nod to the nautical history of the place. It's a space to relax, pause and unwind and take in the art and history of the island. My favourite spot is under the shade of the olive trees in Cantina, the restaurant where they serve authentic Menorcan cuisine, feeling the salty sea breeze with a cold drink in my hand – bliss.

Louise Bourgeois, Spider

+

a nod to its past as a former hospital

Cantina restaurant

Babylonstoren

lemons hang from the ceiling in the restaurant

wine is stored in amphora vessels

In the heart of the Franschhoek Valley north of Stellenbosch you will find the Babylonstoren estate. Babylonstoren has it all: rooms to stay in, a winery, gardens and restaurants, and it is one of the oldest (but also very modern) Cape Dutch working farms. It was purchased by the former editor of *Elle Decoration* South Africa, Karen Roos, and her husband who decided they needed to share this retreat with the world.

The couple have made the most of their location, growing more than 300 plants on the site including vines, fruits and vegetables, along with special collections of cycads and palms, and camomile lawns. Each variety is medicinal or edible, from mulberries to turmeric, and planned meticulously to ensure there are fruits and vegetables year round. The stunning gardens were designed by French landscape designer Patrice Taravella.

You can go on any number of tours to see how the ingredients, including their own honey, olive oil and balsamic vinegar, are lovingly produced. It's hard to think of anything they don't raise themselves and if they don't make it, they source it locally. They even grow their own honeybush and rooibos teas.

The estate is immaculate and the whitewashed farmhouse and buildings are full of rustic charm. Karen's keen eye ensures effortlessly tasteful interiors with neutral palettes, vast four-posters and billowing drapes are enhanced with modern touches. We haven't even started to talk about the wine … pour me a glass, please!

huge varieties of tomatoes are grown & served here

enjoy a Bitterlekker drink

they grow purple potatoes named Adirondack blue

prickly pears

Wormsley

- it's like a secret garden

Wormsley, in the leafy Chiltern Hills, is a much-loved private family estate, acquired in 1985 by Sir Paul Getty. I was lucky enough to have a private tour of the estate, including the library, which houses hundreds of first editions, each with the prettiest of leather bindings. The ceiling here is extraordinary, too, painted in a striking cobalt blue with a chart of the constellation of stars the day Sir Paul was born.

A winding drive leads through the estate and the first stop is the iconic mock-Tudor cricket pavilion with its cricket-bat balustrades. It has been dubbed 'one of the most beautiful cricket grounds in England' and I can see why – even I (not a cricket aficionado) could happily spend an afternoon here sipping Pimm's and enjoying the scenery. A working red telephone box adds a touch of nostalgic charm.

Wormsley is also home to Garsington Opera, providing joyful entertainment for two months of every year. It is housed in an impressive contemporary pavilion by Robin Snell and Partners that sits in the deer park, slightly raised and accessed by a footbridge. This serene, light-filled space often houses exhibitions and private events. Art installations are dotted around the grounds, including pieces by Damien Hirst, Barry Flanagan and Tristano di Robilant.

fern leaf (picked here)

The grounds here are almost magical, with impeccably managed herds of deer and sheep. The wildflower meadow with orange poppies is a wonder. The best spot by far for me, however, is the greenhouse brimming with life, with the ceilings bursting with blooms drying in the warm air. In the walled gardens, with red brickwork and huge doors drawing you in, you feel as if you have jumped straight into a Beatrix Potter book. With the red kites flying overhead, it's hard not to fall in love with Wormsley.

red brick pathways lead through the walled garden

The Island Pavilion

The library

Wormsley

Garsington Opera Pavilion

Ceiling in Library

— they even have an old telephone box

The Cricket Pavilion

The Walled Garden

poppy meadows,

British Pullman

pretty lamp shades on every table

— Cygnus carriage

porcelain china

All aboard! The British Pullman is the UK part of the Venice Simplon-Orient-Express network. It exudes charm, glamour and heritage, and is a unique part of railway history. Feeling as if I were stepping back in time, I clambered on with my travel watercolour set in hand, pondering who had set foot here before me. It's a huge privilege to travel on the British Pullman and I spent a day on the route from London to Whitstable on the Kent coast. Each carriage is in pristine condition, preserving its traditions and original features. The staff greet you with stories of the guests they have welcomed; one recalls the exact seat number and carriage that Nelson Mandela travelled in in 1997 (seat 20, Vera carriage). It was felt that this was the best carriage for him, with the walls adorned in jumping springbok marquetry (panelling).

Once on board you are greeted with a pale blue miniature teacup of cherry wine and encouraged to sit back and relax in the roomy wingback armchairs. These are proper chairs, not the kind you find bolted to the floor of a train, and upholstered in an array of Liberty print fabrics. They are so roomy, in fact, that the train windows had to be taken out to get them in. Details count here; acorn brass tops to the table lampshades, the prettiest glass wall sconces, white peach Bellinis – it's all divine.

brass light fittings

— cherry wine served in tiny tea cups

— acorn detail on the lampshade

Each legendary car has a story to tell, taking the traveller back in time, and some were even named after the designer's wife (such as Audrey and Vera). Each has its own style, unique marquetry and colour palette with exquisite details and motifs. There are mosaic floors with intricate patterns relating to the theme of each and some are even signed by the mosaic artist Aimée in the sweetest way with a little bee. My favourite part of the journey was walking through each carriage as we entered a tunnel; in the atmospheric darkness I could almost imagine myself back in time, lit by Art Deco wall lights, wearing a flapper dress and with a shiny cocktail in hand. A remarkable experience I would definitely love to repeat.

mosaic flooring

Highlights of each incredible carriage

Audrey – often used to convey members of the Royal Family, the carriage has 12 panels of landscape marquetry

Cygnus – Australian walnut, redesigned by Wes Anderson and featured here

Gwen – feminine palette of blues and gold with pearwood motifs on English walnut

Ibis – strong and classic with Liberty-print armchairs and Greek dancing figures

Ione – elegant and soft with burr wood panels and Victorian flora

Lucille – Grecian urns and green veneer with wafts of greys and pinks

Minerva – Edwardian refinement with discreet marquetry and tapestry

Perseus – Ash panels and natural shades of green and cream with a display of old prints

Phoenix – lively bright blue upholstery and Art Deco elegance

Vera – 1930s sandalwood with a mahogany border, springboks and palms in browns and gold

Zena – Art Deco in soft browns and pinks with octagonal mirrors

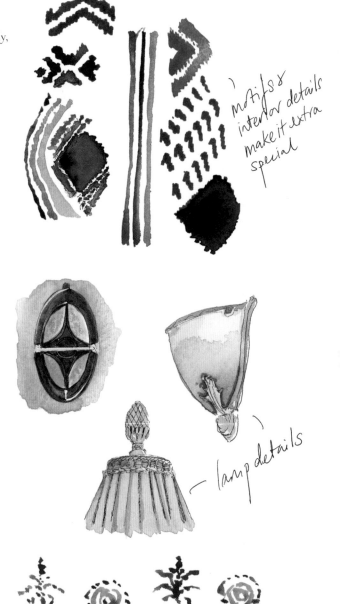

motifs & interior details make it extra special

lamp details

Charleston

As you drive to Charleston, at the end of a country lane in the East Sussex countryside, it's as if you are going to visit friends. This is where Vanessa Bell and Duncan Grant brought members of the Bloomsbury Group together to share their love of art and ideals. Frequented by the most influential artists, writers and prominent creatives and intellectuals of the time, its interior is home to over 60 years of artistic creativity.

the light casts shadowy wisps like clouds on the ceiling

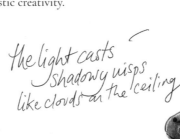

hand painted mural above the mantle & stencilled walls

Virginia Woolf introduced her sister Vanessa Bell to the area in 1916 and encouraged her to move there. Having seen pictures of the house many times, I felt as if I had already visited, but nothing prepared me for the atmosphere of the place. I felt quite emotional imagining the creativity and conversation that went on between these walls. The tour starts in the kitchen and the first thing that you notice is the handmade ceramic and bead lightshade. Based on a Turkish lamp design, it's a sort of upside-down colander and the holes cast a charming light, like wisps of cloud, onto the ceiling. Handmade tiles surround the sink and behind the Aga, and familiar collections of pottery are displayed on the shelves. There is a large cupboard hand painted with fruit and vases of flowers, and a collection of pottery mugs hangs on the wall as if they have recently been used. The whole place feels deeply personal, as if you are sneaking around someone else's house admiring all their things.

dining room —

Clive's bedroom left and
Vanessa's room above

What I remember most about Vanessa's bedroom are
the walls, roughly painted in the most exquisite way,
mimicking the sky at dusk with every hue imaginable
from softest peach to pale lilacs and blues. The straw
hat she wore for painting is placed poignantly on her
bed. Clive Bell's bedroom, formerly Vanessa's studio,
features a charming band of lemon yellow on the
beams, a cheerful addition to the ochre walls.

cups hang on the walls
of the kitchen ready
to be filled with tea

The dining room, illustrated on page 41, has the prettiest floral chintz curtains and geometric sponge-stencilled walls, which were done with hand-mixed paints of chalk and powdered pigment. The sociable, round hand-painted table, laid as if ready for guests to arrive, stands in the centre, with red lacquer cane chairs designed by Roger Fry for the Omega workshop. A variety of ceramics including a triangular cruet made by Quentin Bell and decorated by Vanessa adorns the middle of the table.

After dinner everyone would retire to the comfort of the garden room (left) and meander through the French doors to the garden. The paisley pattern was stencilled on the walls and white flowers added by hand. The fish rug was designed by Duncan Grant in the 1920s and the room once housed one of the first Picassos in a British private collection. When it had to be sold, Quentin, the son of Clive and Vanessa Bell, painted a copy that still hangs in its place today.

Charleston is a treasure of a place like no other, it will inspire and no doubt awaken a desire to hand paint almost every surface of your own home, too.

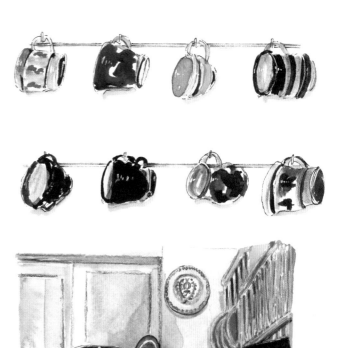

garden room

kitchen with printed
skirt curtain to hide pots

Shell Grotto

razorshell

whelk

There are numerous tales of how the Grade I listed grotto was discovered, but this is the version I prefer. In 1835, when carrying out work in their garden in Margate, Kent, the owners stumbled across a large piece of stone. When it was moved, they couldn't believe their eyes – they were looking down into what resembled an underground temple, covered in shells. I first came across the grotto on a trip to Margate and have been back several times, as the place astounds me. I love, more than anything, that it was hidden beneath the earth for such a long time before it was discovered. I also enjoy its proximity to an area of dense housing. It is baffling how it exists here underground, accessed quite unexpectedly through the grotto shop.

The shell mosaics cover almost 190 square metres and are tarnished with deposits from gas lamps, so they look blackened; it's hard to imagine how stunning this would look with the shells' natural colours. Over 4.6 million stud the walls and they are a mixture of mussels, whelks, oysters, cockles, limpets and razor shells, with a few exotic ones thrown in for good measure. A must-visit if you are in sunny Margate – it really is a wonder.

cockle

oyster

limpet

mussell

Sailors' valentines
The grotto's shop has myriad shell paraphernalia including my favourite sailors' valentines on display. This tradition dates back to the 1800s and the story goes that they were made by sailors to give to their sweethearts. A centrepiece, often based on the shape of a compass or heart, is surrounded by a collage of shells in a complex pattern within an octagonal frame. Here are some of my own hand-painted versions, inspired by Alexandra Tolstoy's collection of antique sailors' valentines.

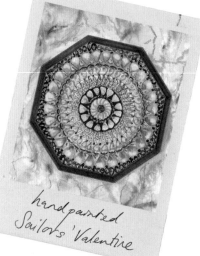

hand painted
Sailors' Valentine

Hotel Cipriani

A five-minute trip on the hotel's shuttle across the lagoon from St Mark's Square brings you to the island of Giudecca, the home of the iconic Hotel Cipriani. The hotel is rendered in a soft pinky hue, 'Bellini pink', named after the colour of the famous drink that was created here by Giuseppe Cipriani in 1948.

Wow, this place is something else. A spot of calm away from the bustle of Venice, discreet, impeccable and charming, this hotel is hard not to fall for. It is all about the details: the lobby with its classic wooden pigeonholes for keys, the antique tiled fireplaces and cheerful Murano glass chandeliers. As you walk through the corridors lined with photographs and hand-written notes from celebrities who have stayed here, you feel part of something very special. The gardens are a peaceful paradise with arches of wisteria leading you to art installations that change with the seasons. The swimming pool area is vast – they built an Olympic-size pool through a planning miscommunication, and it's huge! It feels like the beating heart of the hotel. Guests laze under the brown-and-white parasols that dance in the breeze, sipping on the celebrated Bar Gabbiano cocktails. Rooms are elegant and refined – think understated glamour – and nothing is too much trouble. It's a world like no other and I cannot wait to return.

a room with a heavenly canal view

elegant bedrooms with coloured glass chandeliers

Bellini (serves 1)

60ml/2 fl oz white peach purée
120m/4 fl oz Prosecco

Pour the peach purée into a chilled flute, fill with Prosecco and stir. A layer of foam will naturally form on the top to decorate your drink.

the famous Cipriani shuttle boat that takes you over to St Mark's Square

Cristine Bedfor

This maximalist boutique hotel has an English bed and breakfast feel to it. Centrally located in the bustling hub of Mahón, Menorca, it is crammed with tasteful antiques and vivid textiles. It feels like a home from home and it's definitely all about the interiors here. Hosted by Cristine Bedfor and designed by the brilliant Lorenzo Castillo, rooms of greens, blues and reds are filled with rustic finds and hand-embroidered sheets from Bassols, one of the oldest manufacturers in Europe. Brightly coloured hand-painted furniture, lined with fabric remnants, adds character, and wall plinths provide an intriguing and fun display space for flea-market ceramics. Watercolour paintings of birds and pots in colourful frames and fabric mounts adorn the walls, and collections of antique plates line the hallways. All the senses are considered here, with the heavenly scent of the hotel's own-brand candles and the softest blankets to snuggle up in.

heavenly candles

prettiest plates

coloured glasses

A moment of calm from busy Mahón can be found in the gardens of the hotel, with the pool providing an oasis to cool off in or a restful place to sip a signature cocktail. Every element has been carefully curated to make a relaxed atmosphere throughout, helping you to recharge and restore. It's a truly special place to stay.

clever plinths to display quirky ceramics

Daylesford Organic

On a slightly dreary Sunday, or indeed any free day, there is nothing more I love to do (apart from find a car-boot sale) than jump in the car and pop to Daylesford for the day. Nestled in the heavenly Cotswolds countryside, Daylesford is an organic retreat with a farm shop, multiple cafés and restaurants, homewares and gardening stores, the Bamford Wellness spa and outdoor spaces to relax in with your dog. Thought and care has gone into the carefully chosen products here, each adding value in some small way whether brightening a room or making a task less tiresome. Somehow everything feels better at Daylesford, a real treat; it's a healthy reset for every aspect of living.

the prettiest tableware I ever did see

The greenhouse is a wonderful sanctuary with near-perfect plants and trees to take home. From white wisteria arches to pots of lavender and herbs, there is something here for every gardener. The home store is a mix of rustic finds and neutral pieces, and from oversized woven-grass lighting to effortlessly curated table settings, it's hard not to spend a fortune. The cafés offer a feast of seasonal organic goodness, including homemade pizzas and botanical cocktails. The Daylesford Virgin Mary is my favourite, made with their own tomato juice, horseradish and lemon. It's sure to put a spring back in your step.

large woven lampshades create a relaxed feel

the heady scent of lavender stirs the senses

FIG LEAF
daylesford

festoon lights are
strung from the trees

Chateau Léoube

This vineyard and olive grove in Provence shares the same sustainable, organic principles as Daylesford (and the same owners). The estate includes Café Léoube, situated on Pellegrin beach and surrounded by pine trees – a perfect spot to enjoy an organic Mediterranean lunch and a glass of Léoube rosé. White cotton sheets are suspended from the trees to provide shade from the dry summer heat and salty sea breeze. The olive trees at Léoube (all 4,700) have provided generations with olive oil from varieties including Olivette, Aglandau and Bouteillan. Both the wine and oils are available at Daylesford in the UK so you can experience your own piece of Provence at home.

– sheets
provide a shady
spot

Léoube
rosé wine
is divine
♡

home produce
is served under the olive trees

The Fife Arms

— handpainted ceiling inspired by agate

For an authentic Highland experience created by the genius duo Iwan and Manuela Wirth of Hauser & Wirth, look no further than The Fife Arms in Braemar. This sophisticated hotel places a solid footprint in the dramatic Grampian mountains, just a few miles from Balmoral. Russell Sage Studio (known for their work at The Savoy and The Goring), alongside a team from Moxon Architects, reinvented this imposing Victorian coaching inn, restoring its original splendour. The majesty of the nearby Cairngorms seems to imbue the very floorboards; the light and colours of the landscape dance inside the hotel. It's the perfect base from which to explore the surrounding ancient castles, whisky distilleries, wild walks, breathtaking views, fishing and shooting before coming 'home' to kick off your walking boots and warm your toes at the fender. The gardens at Fife are notable, too. Designed by Jinny Blom, who was tasked with creating a space that reflected the playful, eclectic interior of the hotel, they include winding pathways and plenty of nooks and crannies to explore, grasses and authentic Victorian planting that sits happily with the backdrop of the heather hillside.

William Morris prints

homemade berry jam with scones

tartan blankets to snuggle under

I first stumbled upon Fife through an article in House & Garden magazine. Enthralled by the majestic drawing-room ceiling, I wanted to find out more. The Scottish narrative is strong here – the walls are adorned with the Fife Arms' own tartan designed by Araminta Campbell, and it also drenches the huge wooden sash windows in heavy swags. The traditional look is juxtaposed with exciting modern additions, for example the drawing-room ceiling painted by Chinese artist Zhang Enli and called Ancient Quartz. Zhang took inspiration from Scottish agates, whose deceptively simple exteriors hide a dazzling array of texture and colour inside. You simply cannot miss afternoon tea here – order a decadent cream tea complete with Fife Arms berry jams and sink into the sumptuous sofas and William Morris cushions. Don't forget to look up to admire Zhang's modern masterpiece.

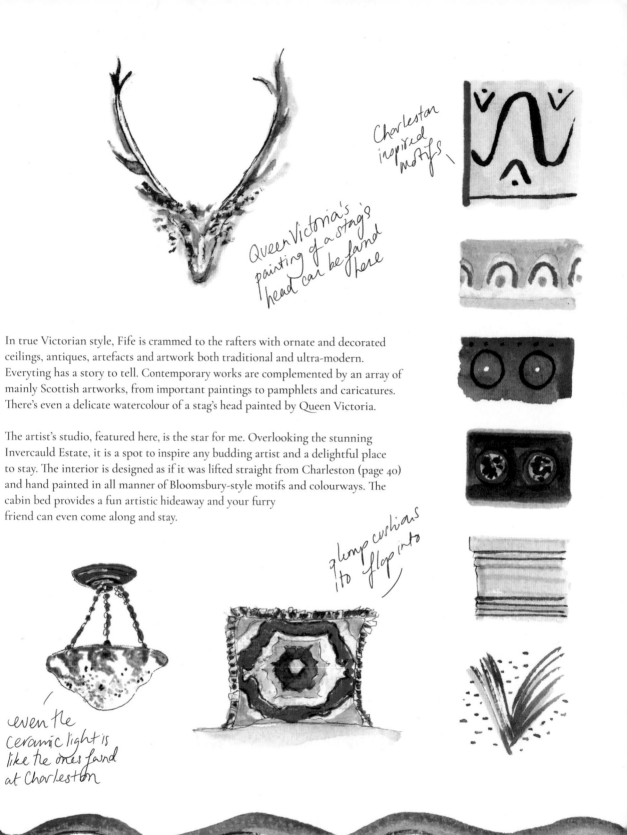

Charleston inspired motifs

Queen Victoria's painting of a stag's head can be found here

In true Victorian style, Fife is crammed to the rafters with ornate and decorated ceilings, antiques, artefacts and artwork both traditional and ultra-modern. Everyting has a story to tell. Contemporary works are complemented by an array of mainly Scottish artworks, from important paintings to pamphlets and caricatures. There's even a delicate watercolour of a stag's head painted by Queen Victoria.

The artist's studio, featured here, is the star for me. Overlooking the stunning Invercauld Estate, it is a spot to inspire any budding artist and a delightful place to stay. The interior is designed as if it was lifted straight from Charleston (page 40) and hand painted in all manner of Bloomsbury-style motifs and colourways. The cabin bed provides a fun artistic hideaway and your furry friend can even come along and stay.

plump cushions ito flop into

even the ceramic light is like the ones found at Charleston

El Fenn

rose petals can be found in the fountains

traditional brass lanterns hang gaily on the walls

This is a place I've dreamed of painting, having seen its colourful interiors featured so often on social media. Owned by Vanessa Branson and Howell James, this Moroccan hotel consisting of thirteen interconnecting riads is tucked down an alleyway next to Bab El Ksour in the heart of Marrakech. When the duo first stumbled across these buildings their vision was to create a feeling of a home away from home, and they certainly succeeded. It has personality, vibrancy and life – and interiors to dream about for days.

It's all about colour here, designed with the expert help of partners Madeline Weinrib and husband Graham Head; every corner of this hotel will wow you with its original and bespoke detailing. Each room has its own palette, from dusty pinks and topaz green to Yves Klein blue, making a relaxed mix with lots of personality. The furnishings were custom-made for each space by local craftsmen, and are combined with jolts of contemporary art and vintage finds; the mix is heavenly.

Décor lovers will adore it all, from fountains of red rose petals to vast collections of bowls adorning the hand-plastered walls, red-and-white striped seating with plump cushions, geometric, ikat and Moroccan prints, rattan and wicker furnishings, floating trays of candles on the pool, walls of hanging lanterns, bright panes of stained glass ... I could go on forever about the design details here.

At the end of the day, with the scent of jasmine and the sounds of the evening call to prayer in the air, head to the rooftop bar to soak up the sunset and an El Fenn margarita ... utter bliss.

stained glass panels add a pop of colour

El Fenn Margarita (serves 1)
1 part hibiscus-infused syrup
1 part tequila
1 part lime juice
fresh ginger juice, to taste

Mix together, shake and serve at sunset.

rooms here have their own palette from dusty pinks, greens & blues

Gracy's

relax with a game of snooker at their full-size table

flag of Malta

I was first introduced to Gracy's Arts and Supper Club (consisting of bar, brasserie and private members' club) by Francis Sultana, a designer I follow avidly. I was thrilled to see another of his transformations here. As an Ambassador for Culture for Malta, native Sultana was the perfect choice for this renovation; he is also involved with Malta's latest museum space, MICAS. Gracy's sits in the heart of the capital Valletta, overlooking St George's Square. It is housed in the stunning, Baroque, 17th-century Palazzo Verdelin (formerly a Civil Service Club), one of Malta's finest national monuments. Sultana adds his usual sense of style; charm with echoes of the past can be felt throughout.

Perched on a hilly peninsula, Valletta (one of Europe's smallest cities) is steeped in history. Built by the Knights of St John in the 16th Century, it is laced with ornate architecture, sloping streets, hundreds of Maltese balconies and statues of saints, so it is well worth a meander.

The Gracy's building has one of the most stunning façades in Malta, extending over three floors. With jaw-dropping rooftop gardens and the beautiful private function room of Salon de Nobile, this is the place to hang or host an event. Chef Tom Peters completes a winning team, ensuring the food is as good as the interior. There is one super-fun space, which must not be missed: the bespoke private karaoke room! It feels like a tube-train carriage with the geometric seating covers extending to line the walls and the ceiling, creating the most incredible acoustics if the microphone is in the right hands. Be warned, though – if you misbehave, Valletta police station is conveniently located next door, so be sure to be on your best behaviour.

puddings to savour

bespoke karaoke room

Halcyon House

Despite topping the list of Australia's best beaches in recent years, Cabarita Beach retains a sleepy hideaway character, nestled on the stunning Tweed Coast in New South Wales. Boutique hotel Halcyon House, sitting on this sandy strip of paradise, is well named. The vibe of the hotel is nostalgic, peaceful, idyllic and happy. Once a classic 1960s surf motel, it's low-key yet stylish, reminiscent of both Palm Springs and the Hamptons but ultimately very Aussie, a combination of your best childhood beachside holidays and barefoot laid-back living. Owner sisters Siobhan and Elisha Bickle have made the most of its location and transformed it into a destination for the design conscious. If you are looking to escape to a slice of heaven, this is your place.

palm motif found on towels to notebooks

enjoy a cocktail or two

lots of goodies to be found in the Halcyon Atelier shop

sumptuous bedroom designed by Anna Spiro

One of my favourite Australian designers, Anna Spiro, has created individual looks for each of the 19 rooms and three suites with her signature style mixing vintage furnishings, upholstered or papered walls, strong colours and graphic patterns. Sublime collections of prints and paintings are clustered on bold walls. Brass sconces, lots of books, plumped cushions, painted wooden floors and embroidered headboards combine to create a distinctive, elegant and homely feel. No room has the same look or layout and private balconies, patios and courtyards all have spectacular views. A fresh blue and white motif runs through the hotel, with an abundance of clam-shell shapes to remind you where you are. This is definitely somewhere you can forget about your troubles.

restful places to relax in

Sketch

fun hopscotch in the entrance lobby

the lighting is simply stunning in every space

battenburg with tea

Sketch can be found in a Georgian townhouse on Conduit Street, just off London's Regent Street. The creation of restaurateur Mourad Mazouz, this is a hub of multiple bars and restaurants, each with its own distinct theme. When I visited, the first thing I noticed was the playful hopscotch on the floor at the entrance. It sets the tone and lets you know that there is fun to be had here. This is an art-led establishment where the walls are constantly evolving with new installations and artists showcased.

First stop on the ground floor is the Parlour, the most relaxed space, a quirky tea room by day that morphs into a cocktail bar at night. The Gallery, with pastel-pink walls and soft yellow, marshmallow-like seating was a collaboration between designer India Mahdavi and artist Yinka Shonibare, and the Africa-inspired artworks here are a wonder. Scented by Diptyque's Cypress candles, this is the perfect spot for a refined afternoon tea with live classical music. You will be served miniature delights from Battenberg to scones and advised by your own tea master.

enjoy pink drinks

The Lecture Room and Library are the real gems here for me. The showstopping décor matches up to the food, which has won three Michelin stars. Designed by Gabhan O'Keeffe, this opulent room with silvery, ivory walls boasts crimson and orange upholstered seating and a sunburst pink and ochre-toned carpet. A scarlet chandelier hangs majestically from the frescoed ceiling – with lilac tassels and trim, it is out of this world.

macarons

The Glade at Sketch (right) is bewitching, an enchanted fairytale of a place, like walking into a magical forest. Your first experience is underfoot, where a hand-woven carpet squishes beneath your toes, emulating a mossy floor. There is violet and cobalt blue plush velvet seating, and chandeliers hanging from tree branches. You will be dazzled by the theatre of it all.

The sunken futuristic East bar is a real escape-from-reality experience. I particularly love the Faber-Castell pencils lined up on the bar counter. The dome above the bar, designed by Noé Duchaufour-Lawrance and covered in graffiti, is brilliant and I was desperate to add something to it (note that I didn't!). And the egg-shaped pod loos, beneath a ceiling of backlit coloured tiles, steal the show – this spot has possibly been snapped and posted more than any other toilet in London. The regular exhibition installations here make the loos the coolest of places to hang out.

I Bethan Gray pop up painted by my Mummy for @roomportraitclub

grafitti in the bar

eggshaped loos with coloured glass ceiling - an experience in itself

John Derian

handmade
paper
plants

I first fell in love with John Derian's work when I lived in California in the early 2000s, so it was serendipitous to stumble across his homewares store nestled among the delights of New York's West Village on a recent visit. With distressed paintwork and a Parisian vibe, this charming store is a treasure trove of ceramics, textiles and an homage to John's signature decoupage work.

The John Derian Company was formed in the 1980s when, inspired by his own collection of 18th- and 19th-century botanical, fruit and animal prints, he developed a range of decoupage pieces, now much coveted by avid fans around the world. This art of cutting and pasting paper finds its way onto almost any type of object here, from paperweights, trays and vases to plates, all made lovingly by John's team of artisans.

heart
charm
collaged
paper
under
hand blown
glass

pretty
matches

marbled
plates

The store itself is a jewel-box of a place, crammed with cubbyholes brimming with decorative objects for the home. The building, a former pet shop, has been restored to transport you back in time – even the wallpaper was given a faded finish to make it look like it had been sunkissed over time, and it's easy to imagine that this place has been here forever. It has the most darling shell-studded original fireplace and paper plants, and flowers by Livia Cetti dotted about add life and colour. John's curation of items feels nostalgic and precious; they are heirlooms to pass onto future generations.

Heckfield Place

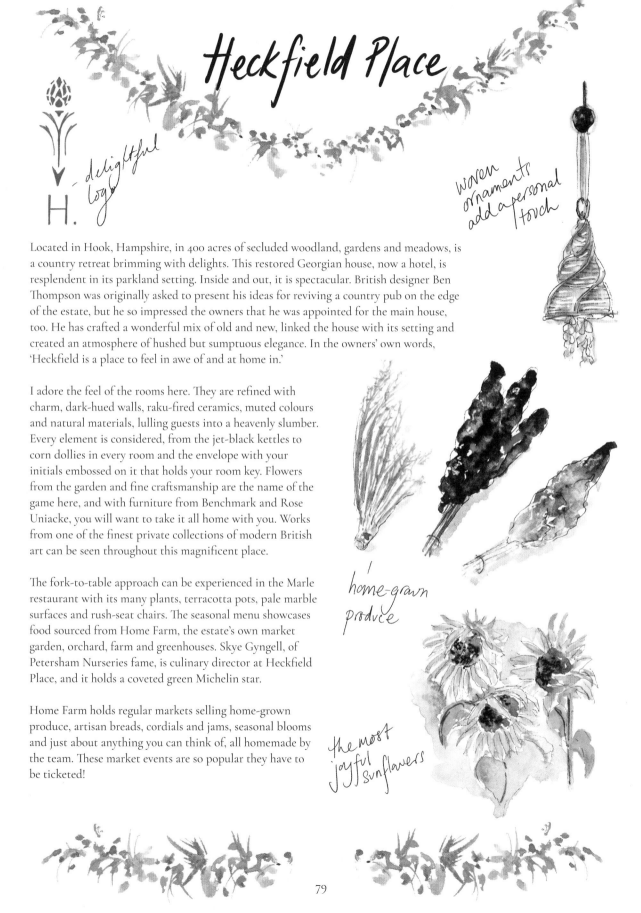

H. — delightful logo

woven ornaments add a personal touch

Located in Hook, Hampshire, in 400 acres of secluded woodland, gardens and meadows, is a country retreat brimming with delights. This restored Georgian house, now a hotel, is resplendent in its parkland setting. Inside and out, it is spectacular. British designer Ben Thompson was originally asked to present his ideas for reviving a country pub on the edge of the estate, but he so impressed the owners that he was appointed for the main house, too. He has crafted a wonderful mix of old and new, linked the house with its setting and created an atmosphere of hushed but sumptuous elegance. In the owners' own words, 'Heckfield is a place to feel in awe of and at home in.'

I adore the feel of the rooms here. They are refined with charm, dark-hued walls, raku-fired ceramics, muted colours and natural materials, lulling guests into a heavenly slumber. Every element is considered, from the jet-black kettles to corn dollies in every room and the envelope with your initials embossed on it that holds your room key. Flowers from the garden and fine craftsmanship are the name of the game here, and with furniture from Benchmark and Rose Uniacke, you will want to take it all home with you. Works from one of the finest private collections of modern British art can be seen throughout this magnificent place.

The fork-to-table approach can be experienced in the Marle restaurant with its many plants, terracotta pots, pale marble surfaces and rush-seat chairs. The seasonal menu showcases food sourced from Home Farm, the estate's own market garden, orchard, farm and greenhouses. Skye Gyngell, of Petersham Nurseries fame, is culinary director at Heckfield Place, and it holds a coveted green Michelin star.

Home Farm holds regular markets selling home-grown produce, artisan breads, cordials and jams, seasonal blooms and just about anything you can think of, all homemade by the team. These market events are so popular they have to be ticketed!

home-grown produce

the most joyful sunflowers

HR Giger Bar Museum

If you are seeking an immersive art experience, look no further than the HR Giger Bar in the medieval town of Gruyères, Switzerland. Swiss-born H. R. Giger was an acclaimed biomechanical artist whose work explored the connection between human and machine forms, and the bar here is an immersive display of Giger's biomechanical style. The roof, walls, fittings and even the chairs were modelled by the artist over a period of two years before its opening in February 1992. The bar itself is like a cave, with the roof held up by criss-crossing arches of vertebrae. These skeletal ceiling panels were created in rubber moulds in his studio and cast in fibreglass (earlier prototypes in cement were too heavy). Giger designed every other detail of the bar, from the oval mirrors to the wall lamps and even the coat racks. The chair design was originally intended for a throne in the famously abandoned 1975 film project 'Dune', and continued to be a part of his signature style, with an elegant curve and rounded 'swoosh' shape, tapered legs and high back. His work has an ecclesiastical air to it and is rather macabre, but fascinates me nonetheless.

Next door to the bar is the HR Giger Museum, set up by Giger following a successful exhibition at the Chateau de Gruyères. This was his chance to create a permanent home for his work and it is maintained to this day. The museum and bar together make for a delightful day out.

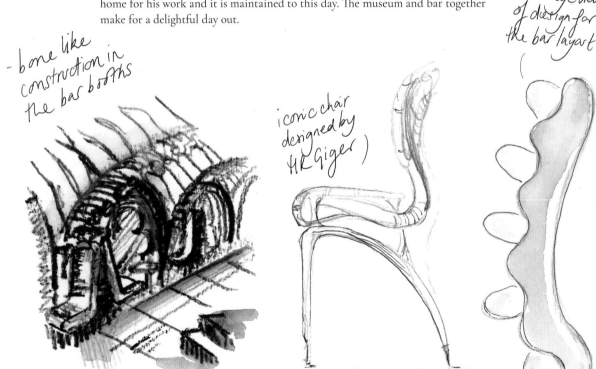

– bone like construction in the bar booths

iconic chair designed by HR Giger)

bird's eye view of design for the bar layout (

Monet's House

Claude Monet was the first artist I really loved. Aged about 13 I spent all my pocket money on a book of his paintings, poring over every page. His giant waterlilies moved me to tears on a recent visit to the Musée de l'Orangerie in Paris, so it is wonderful to feature his home here. I was familiar with his famous waterlily gardens and it was exciting to learn that his house is equally astounding. He resided here in Giverny, Normandy, from 1883 to 1926, with his second wife Alice Hoschedé and their combined eight children, so it was a lively household indeed. Called 'House of the Cider Press', it was extended over time to suit the family's needs. It is a very long building now, pink-hued with emerald-green shutters, but only five metres deep.

Monet meticulously hand picked every colour in the house, each working in harmony or in contrast with the next. Two rooms really stand out to me; the first is the yellow dining room featured here, which is extraordinary, bearing in mind that it was created in the 19th Century when the fashion was for dark and austere interiors (see Sambourne House, page 164). This is the opposite in every way. Almost everything is covered in the most jubilant yellow, from painted chairs to tables and cabinets. Some of Monet's Japanese engravings adorn the walls, part of a huge hoard he collected over 50 years. The red-and-white tiled flooring serves to make the yellow even brighter, and green vases provide bold accents of contrast. I can only imagine the fun of dinner parties here, all observed by the resident Japanese biscuitware cat.

Monet had a vast
Japanese print
collection

Japanse
biscuitware
cat

palette of yellow, red & green

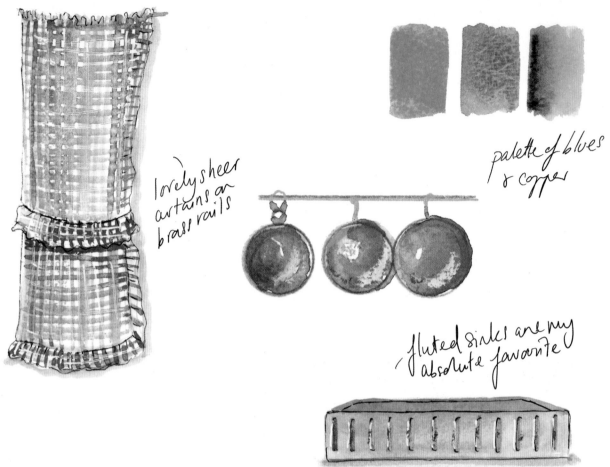

lovely sheer curtains on brass rails

palette of blues & copper

fluted sinks are my absolute favourite

Rouen tiles)

Adjoining the dining room, the kitchen is equally striking. Monet wanted a blue kitchen to balance and harmonise with the yellow of the dining room and it does just that, it's a cool, calming space that feels fresh and light. There are numerous blue tones from turquoise to inky blues found in the Rouen tiles. Walls are covered in the tiles from floor to ceiling, with copper pots displayed from brass poles. The copper creates a warm glow offset by the blue hues; this is as carefully curated as his paintings.

Monet's studio was in a barn next door, self-contained with an apartment upstairs. Although he preferred to paint in the open air (*en plein air*), he stored his canvases and paints here. Spring is a great time to visit – with a sea of tulip beds and carpets of hyacinths in the garden, every sense is inspired and invigorated with colour.

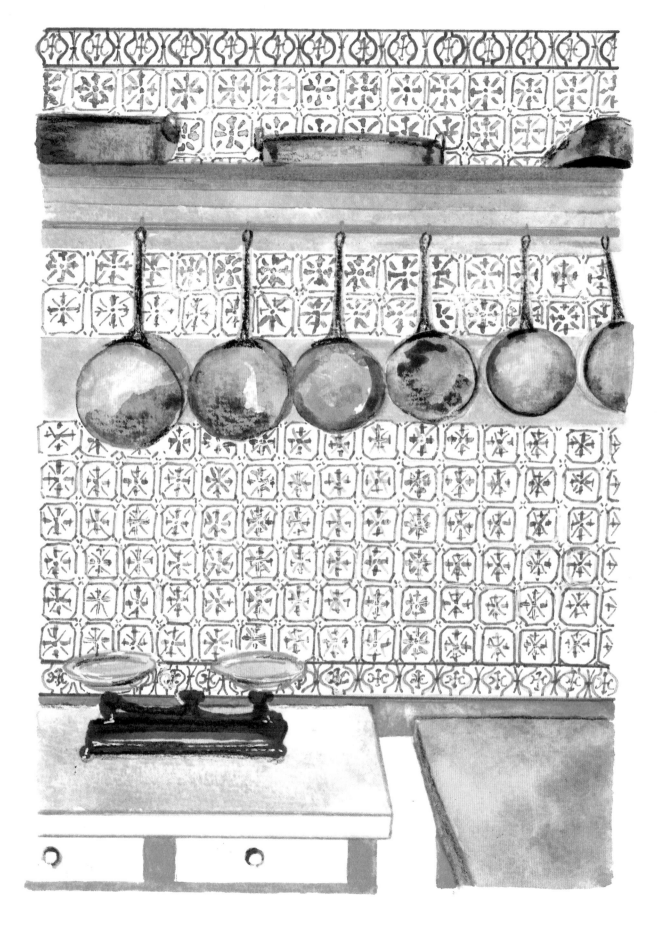

GoldenEye

This exclusive boutique resort in Oracabessa Bay, Jamaica, comprises several villas, cottages and beach huts and is where, at a curved wooden corner desk in a villa that he designed for himself, Ian Fleming wrote all 14 of his James Bond books. Fleming first fell in love with the Caribbean during a visit when he was a naval officer in 1942. He returned after the war and was inspired to create a home here, naming it after an intelligence operation called GoldenEye. He named his iconic character after an English ornithologist and author of *Birds of the West Indies*. Apparently, Fleming was after an ordinary sort of quiet name and he felt that James Bond fitted the bill. Of course, 007 is anything but ordinary and neither is this place.

In 1970, Island Records' founder Chris Blackwell acquired the property and has been sensitively developing it ever since. From beach huts to lagoon cottages and villas, there is an abundance of four-posters, floaty sheer cotton drapes and linen furnishings, and the original Fleming Villa is the jewel in the crown. Secluded in its own lush tropical gardens on the estate, it has a private beach and pool and has been extended to include a media room and two separate cottages. The original villa is still as Fleming designed it allowing the sun and sea breezes to gently blow through the jalousie windows into the light, airy interiors.

The room featured here is the Spanish Elm lagoon hut and one of the first structures that Chris built. Nearby you can spot trees planted by visiting notables, part of a tree-planting scheme where guests can donate to the Oracabessa Foundation, which helps fund sustainable local development. This is a magical place which creative people have visited for years, and I was particularly overjoyed to find out that Sting wrote 'Every Breath You Take' here. This place is definitely on my wish list, with a licence to thrill!

the corner desk where the James Bond books were written

BIRDS OF THE WEST INDIES BY JAMES BOND B.A (CANE.)

inspiration for James Bond's name

GUAVA TREE PLANTED BY ___ JAN 10-96

coral reef preservation is high on the agenda

propagating staghorn coral

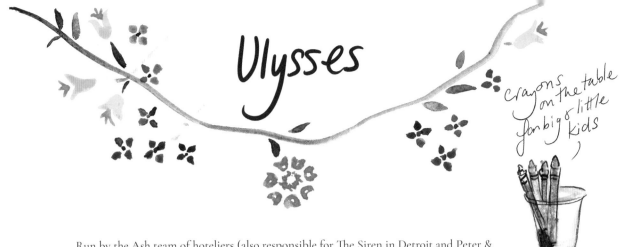

Ulysses

crayons on the table for big & little kids

Run by the Ash team of hoteliers (also responsible for The Siren in Detroit and Peter & Paul in New Orleans), this hotel in Baltimore is an absolute winner. A 1912 Renaissance-style building plays host to this party-vibe hotel with interiors inspired by the art of travel and, as the proprietors say, 'Soft beds and strong drinks' to set the tone. On the Ulysses mood boards were references to James Joyce's novel, *The Greek Adventures of Odysseus* and even a maritime theme via a Bavarian immigrant ship that docked in Baltimore. So you can imagine the delights to be explored once you're inside. This isn't just a hotel for overnight visitors, Ash also wanted to create a space for locals to call home, too.

The Art Deco Ash-Bar is inspired by the Parisian salons of Gertrude Stein, with burl wood panelling encasing the walls and sinuous mouldings creating a seamless look alongside the veneered surfaces. In the bedrooms there is a bold and quirky feel, mixed with a cacophony of pattern and textiles such as the quilted bedspreads featured here, and hints of Indian palaces and Etrurian treasures. Oh, and there is also a nod to the legendary filmmaker John Waters via the odd flamingo motif here and there.

A visit to the cocktail lounge Bloom's, named after the 'hero' of James Joyce's *Ulysses*, Leopold Bloom, is an absolute must. Think bold reds and violets mixed with mirrors on every surface, Deco curves and leopard print and you have the look. Put on your most glitzy jewels, highest heels and sparkle the night away. Nightcaps here are compulsory!

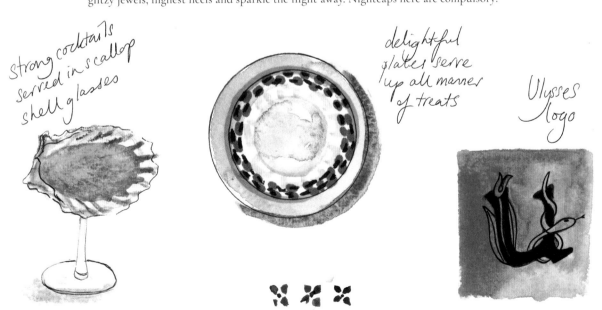

strong cocktails served in scallop shell glasses

delightful plates serve up all manner of treats

Ulysses logo

Chandler House

Michael has reworked the willow pattern design for a wonderful collection of ceramics

Chandler House logo

If you are in Cape Town, South Africa, and love all things antiques, interiors and art, this is the place to go! It is a total gem of a shop and every hand-picked item in it tells a story. London-born ceramicist Michael Chandler, who clearly has an expert eye, shares his carefully curated edit of handcrafted textiles, ceramics, prints, antiques and gifts.

Michael also runs the Voorkamer Gallery, where he regularly features exhibits from talented new artists as well as his own incredible work. The name has its origins in the Afrikaans 'voor' meaning front and 'kamer' room. Traditionally front rooms, especially in Cape Dutch houses or farmhouses, contained the household's most precious pieces and this small gallery displays treasures for visitors to view.

tile mural based on his love of the Cape

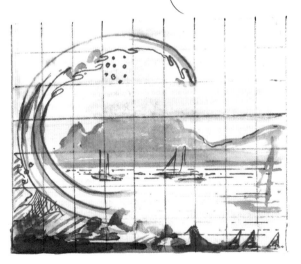

Michael's own ceramic work, created in the upstairs studio, demonstrates his love for the Cape; its architecture, flora, fauna and coastal setting inform many of his pieces. He also creates vast hand-painted tile murals that adorn homes, bars, farms and even chapels. He weaves a story into each very individual piece, including personal references, symbols and motifs.

My favourites are his clever Cape versions of the blue and white willow-pattern china we all know and love. At first glance they look like original designs (which traditionally showed a Chinese scene) but on closer inspection Michael has depicted a legend from the Cape instead. Treasure seekers need look no further.

Horta Museum

If, like me, you are a fan of Art Nouveau, the Horta Museum in Brussels is an absolute must. Owned and designed by the creative genius and much celebrated Belgian architect Victor Horta, this building, completed in 1901, showcases the detail and beauty of the fleeting Art Nouveau movement (1890–1910). A visit here is an invitation into the heart of Horta's own home and studio. Once you've checked your phone in (to avoid careless damage being done if you are concentrating on taking photos rather than the surroundings), you are able to wander the house freely with no barriers or cordoned-off areas. It is also possible to book a private visit. The museum has undergone meticulous restoration and stands much as it would have when it was first built. Horta submitted his first planning application in 1898 and the structure and interior decoration over several floors has been wonderfully preserved. It was the first Art Nouveau listed building in the Brussels region and is a UNESCO World Heritage Site.

As you tiptoe around, the floorboards creak underfoot and you take in the sensuous flowing lines from the ironwork on balconies to the feminine curves in the mosaic floors, carved woodwork and luminous glass ceiling. The soft light is incredible here, creating a sense of space and an ethereal feel. Ornamental designs echo the architectural features of the building, from bedheads to door handles, hinges to lighting, wallpaper to sculpture; every bit of furniture and interior decoration is a glorious example of the artistic movement with which Horta's name is synonymous. Descend the elegant central stairway and be transported to another age.

every inch of the place has charming Art Deco details

Art Deco details

sinuous curves on the staircase banister design

brass lamps & translucent shades

92

Salthrop House

nasturtiums grow happily in the garden

I felt an instant connection to Salthrop House, because it is located in the Wiltshire town of Wroughton, where I was born. The home of designer Sophie Conran, it is set on the edge of the chalky Marlborough Downs, just a hop and a skip away from Avebury (which has a mini, much less touristy, stone henge, and walks to die for). The sweeping driveway lures you in to meet the most charming 200-year-old manor house with soft, buttery-toned bricks and a handsome façade, set in mature, blowsy gardens filled with the prettiest blooms imaginable.

Everything Sophie touches has an effortless feel. Take a short stroll through the vegetable garden, where each raised bed is encased in hand-woven twigs and sticks that protect the plants and look charming, too. Visit the greenhouse, with more than enough room to accommodate Sophie's extensive geranium collection. A huge salt-glazed sink is the perfect spot to wash away the mud and arrange cut flowers. There are chickens pecking around and when I visited, some chicks had just hatched and were blundering around exploring their new world. And what a world to grow up in. I haven't mentioned the house interiors yet ... well proportioned with high ceilings, grand but not intimidating. Most rooms face south and the light dances around, highlighting Sophie's beautiful touches. The kitchen is homely, colourful, eclectic and full of treasured finds. In the dining room I loved the way Sophie had hand stitched antique embroidered linens together to create one vast patchwork cloth to cover the table. Upstairs, rooms are airy and bright with canopy beds, colourful textiles and embroidered panels like the one featured here. I got the full tour – even the boiler cupboard walls are covered in the most darling vintage floral wallpaper. The good news is that you can visit, too, as the house is available for private events and there is often a charity Christmas market, which is a must-add to your calendar.

bed of dreams

The baby chicks hatched the week I visited

La Mère de Famille

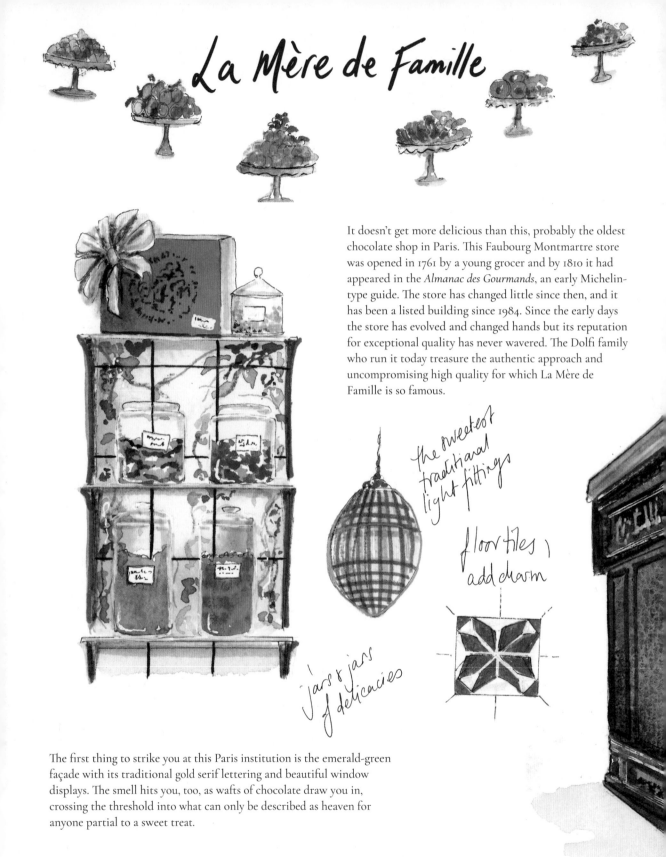

It doesn't get more delicious than this, probably the oldest chocolate shop in Paris. This Faubourg Montmartre store was opened in 1761 by a young grocer and by 1810 it had appeared in the *Almanac des Gourmands*, an early Michelin-type guide. The store has changed little since then, and it has been a listed building since 1984. Since the early days the store has evolved and changed hands but its reputation for exceptional quality has never wavered. The Dolfi family who run it today treasure the authentic approach and uncompromising high quality for which La Mère de Famille is so famous.

the sweetest traditional light fittings

floor tiles add charm

jars & jars of delicacies

The first thing to strike you at this Paris institution is the emerald-green façade with its traditional gold serif lettering and beautiful window displays. The smell hits you, too, as wafts of chocolate draw you in, crossing the threshold into what can only be described as heaven for anyone partial to a sweet treat.

Old mosaic tiles greet you with the company name on the floor, there are shiny mahogany counters and traditional cabinetry, antique ceiling lamps, vintage glass jars, and stands and baskets of exquisitely packaged chocolates and sweets. The owners have preserved the heritage of this iconic brand but also moved with the times, adapting recipes to reduce sugar content for the more health-conscious Parisians of today. They even make their own ice-cream using fresh fruit, macarons are a speciality, too, and every item is exquisitely gift-wrapped in their signature box and tied with the prettiest orange ribbon.

old-style counters display an array of confectionery

Leighton House

– Arab Hall

The former home and studio of Frederic, Lord Leighton is a treasure of a house to visit, just off London's Kensington High Street. It's hard to believe that this interior is tucked away close to such bustling streets. Leighton bought the land in 1864 and developed the house over several years with the help of his architect friend, George Aitchison. The house was inspired by Leighton's travels to Turkey, Syria and Egypt where, like many Victorians, he collected ceramics and objets to display at home. And boy, did he create the place to show off his finds, employing the best craftsmen of the time including ceramicist William De Morgan, artist Walter Crane, sculptor Edgar Boehm and illustrator Randolph Caldecott. It's hard to believe what lies inside the relatively modest red-brick exterior. The majestic Arab Hall, a glittering and opulent turquoise-tiled space that even has a fountain centre stage, was inspired by the interiors of La Zisa, a 12th-century Arab–Norman palace in Palermo, Sicily. It boasts visually astounding friezes with mythical creatures and vines, and many of the tiles that feature here were brought back from Damascus by Leighton. The central, golden-domed ceiling has seen many a sight, as this room was the location of lavish parties for the fashionable artistic society of the day. Leighton surrounded himself with like-minded individuals such as Edward Burne-Jones and James Whistler, and even Queen Victoria visited. The rest of the house is equally enchanting, brimming with art for art's sake, and truly a hidden gem in London not to be missed.

William De Morgan vases to die for on display

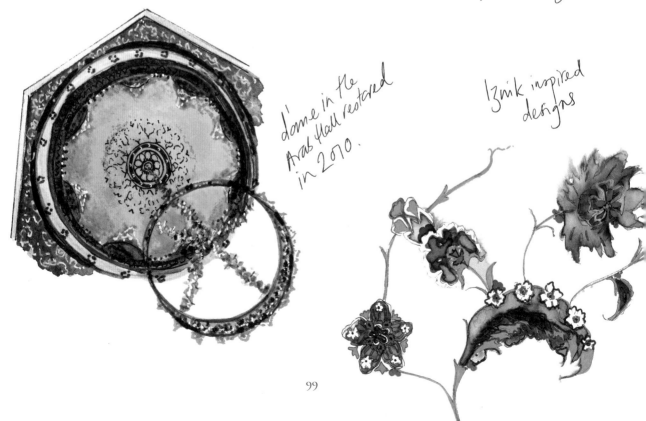

dome in the Arab Hall restored in 2010.

Iznik inspired designs

Hotel les Deux Gares

the entrance is tucked away behind lots of greenery

This charming Parisian hotel is super-close to both Gare du Nord and Gare l'Est and makes a perfect base for exploring Paris. Designed by artist and designer Luke Edward Hall, the period building is brought to life with an electric pea-green lobby that creates a bold first impression and sets the tone for what is beyond. An eclectic mix of subtle *toile de Jouy* wallpapers is paired with strong, punchy-coloured architectural details and geometric floor tiles. Chairs made by Italian architect, Paola Buffa, and leopard-print sofas provide a fun, bohemian space in which to unwind. Gold keys with red tassels await every guest and Bonne Nouvelle toiletries with scents of fresh verbena invigorate you for the day ahead. Luke's paintings adorn the walls of the lobby and the bedrooms have lightshades decorated with his drawings. If you love Luke's style, you will lap up every inch of this place.

The hotel boasts its own café located just around the corner. With its cheerful and welcoming pink and deep red awning, it is the perfect pit stop for coffee en route to the day's sightseeing. Or, as I did, just sit outside at one of the tables that feature Luke's drawings and watch the world go by.

leaf shaped wall sconce

rooms are brimming with bold colour and pattern

Le Sirenuse

This iconic hotel sits high in the cliffs overlooking Positano's pebble beach and the azure sea of the Amalfi coast. The enchanting majolica-tiled dome of Santa Maria Assunta church is a stone's throw away, a highlight of the vista visible through the hotel's vast glass doors. Le Sirenuse's exterior is painted in a rich Cordovan red with white, and their logo shows two mermaids (sirens) holding the hotel high in the sky. The place has a charm and family feel to it, a nod to its past as the seaside home of the aristocratic Sersale family. Each room once had a golden mermaid key that would unlock the delights of antiques and special touches inside (since replaced by more practical key cards, but the gold keys still hang in reception). White and bright rooms greet guests, each unique and filled with thoughtful touches and the family's finds, from colourful suzani cushions to ceramics and art. Franco Sersale kept auction records of the hundreds of beautiful objects he purchased, and his careful eye knew exactly where to place each treasure. Today, Le Sirenuse invites artists from around the world to produce work inspired by the hotel's aesthetic and surrounding panorama, creating a wonderful juxtaposition of old and contemporary work on display. Giant terracotta pots filled with established plants trail the walls inside and out, and the vibrant pink *Bougainvillea* drenches you at night with the heady scent of Summer.

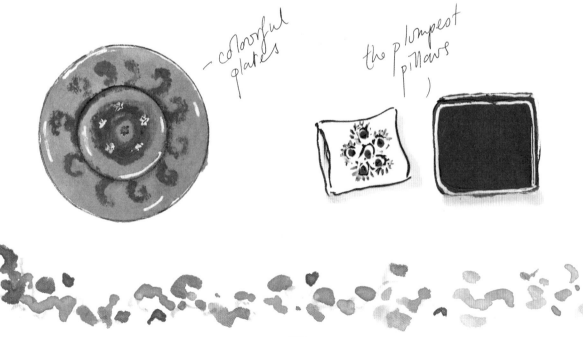

— colourful plates

the plumpest pillows)

famous neo-Baroque yellow fountain

hanging tomatoes ripen in the sun

Franco's bar

With a punchy yellow neo-Baroque fountain paired with Yves-Klein-blue tables and chairs, this is the perfect spot for a proper old-school cocktail done the right way. Stop by for sublime views and an authentic experience that will create memories for a lifetime (they don't take reservations, but it's worth the wait).

Franco's Fizz

ground pistachios mixed with salt
60 ml/2 fl oz almond milk
50 ml/1¾ fl oz Italicus liqueur
15 ml/½ fl oz lemon juice
5 ml/¼ fl oz simple sugar syrup
50 ml/1¾ fl oz lemonade
lemon zest, to garnish

Roll the rim of your glass in ground pistachio and salt before mixing the ingredients and garnishing with a twist of lemon zest.

Franco's fizz served in stripey tumblers

oxblood
exterior
with vines &
palms

Le Sirense
logo, two
mermaids

Caffè Florian

In the heart of Venice you will find Caffè Florian, one of the world's oldest coffee houses, opened in 1720 and much the same today. It's a major tourist spot and very easy to find, as a large crowd gathers to listen to live music from the Caffè Florian Orchestra. Opera and classical pieces serenade those seated at the al-fresco tables spread out under the arches in St Mark's Square in the summer months. This place is a treat; waiters greet you in pristine, traditional black coat-tails and as long as you are up for spending a bit it's the perfect spot to watch the world go by and take in the architecture and ambience of Venice. I ordered a glass of fizz and a tiramisu, which I can safely say were worth every Euro. Several rooms make up the Florian's palatial interior, with glimmering gilt mirrors reflecting paintings that hold centuries of tales. Each room has a theme, including Chinese, Senate, and Liberty rooms, the Room of Seasons, and the Room of the Illustrious Men (celebrated Venetian artists). The marble tables here are elaborate, ornate and full of charm, the seating is plush red velvet, and it's hard to resist the romance of it all.

music serenades you

the most delicious tiramisu

chandeliers overhead

intricate mosaic floor

gilt mirrors add a regal feel

Liberty London

Liberty, one of London's finest department stores, was launched in 1875 by Arthur Lasenby Liberty and the building is called Chesham House after the town he lived in. Chesham happens to be my nearest town, and the Liberty family still live up the road in the next village. Arthur Liberty worked his way up at Farmer and Rogers, a women's fashion business, selling sought-after Japanese shawls to customers including some of the most influential artists of the time. Through this, he formed close relationships with the likes of William Morris, James Whistler and Dante Gabriel Rossetti. His dream was always to own a store of his own and these friends encouraged him to set up. Liberty London soon became a hotspot for Oriental and Arts-and-Craft items. He eventually expanded the business to include furniture and homewares, with Liberty's own textile designs and carefully selected, high-quality imports.

I always Liberty associate with its iconic peacock feather design fabric

archived Liberty wallpaper features in my studio & brings me joy everyday

authentic dial on the lift

divine Iphis design

Liberty prints will forever be some of my most cherished fabric designs, I am always drawn to their bright colours and busy patterns and the sense of nostalgia they evoke. I long to visit the archives, which today inspire new collaborations with the likes of Martina Mondadori's *Cabana* magazine. Liberty originally created their prints by importing plain undyed cottons and silks, and dyeing them in Staffordshire. Before long, the world described the range, which was called 'Art Colours', as 'Liberty colours'. The quality and craftsmanship was second to none and so the Liberty collection was born.

I love exploring the Liberty building with its dark wood-panelled staircases and tiny shiny lifts; it was designed to feel more like wandering through a home rather than a store. Built with Arts-and-Crafts philosophy in mind, ensuring materials and skills are top-notch, it is all still beautifully intact today. The building itself, in Tudor style, is synonymous with the brand and was constructed using timber from decommissioned ships. There are fireplaces in several rooms, with Delft tiles and plasterwork details that add to the appeal. I particularly love the way things are displayed here; for example, plates are displayed upright in wooden shelves so that the pattern can be seen, and I have emulated this carpentry design in my own kitchen at home.

Wood carvings can be spotted throughout the store, from monkeys and bears to frogs on the stairs. The central atrium, with what is claimed to be the longest chandelier in Europe, is the showstopper for me, and I particularly loved seeing giant paper chains strung from floor to floor here at Christmas. Oscar Wilde once said that 'Liberty is the chosen resort of the artistic shopper', and I agree with him wholeheartedly.

this tablescape featured in the Liberty magazine

one Christmas the central atrium was filled with oversized paper chains

Wild at Heart flowers, a must-stop on exit

Dresdner Molkerei Gebrüder Pfund

The Pfund dairy (Dresdner Molkerei Gebrüder Pfund) is like no other. When you arrive at this remarkable store in Dresden, Germany, you could be forgiven for thinking you were visiting a royal palace rather than a shop selling milk products. Its ornate and lavish decoration, from floor to ceiling, is astounding – and was also a huge challenge for me to paint!

Paul Pfund founded the dairy after moving from the countryside to Dresden in 1879 with just six cows, intending to supply fresh milk to the city's citizens. The city was growing rapidly and milk from the surrounding areas was often sour by the time it arrived. In 1892, Paul opened this unique store and by 1895 the company was processing 40,000 litres a day. The building survived two World Wars, forced takeovers and financial mismanagement, but was in a state of disrepair before a descendant of the original Pfund family alerted the Institute for the Preservation of Historical Monuments, which placed it under a preservation order.

Today, the space has been restored to its former glory, with beautiful frosted-glass lights hanging from an ornate ceiling and nearly 300 square metres of tiles produced by artists from Villeroy & Boch adorning every surface. The hand-painted tiles with blue and gold accents depict the dairy's history and much more, featuring cheerful cherubs, children playing, mythical creatures, garlands of flowers, cows chewing the cud and even woodland animals.

For authentic milk, buttermilk and cheese delicacies this place is so special that it was awarded the Guinness World Record for being 'the most beautiful dairy in the world'. It most certainly is.

stunning columns in bold colours

adornments on every surface

tiles restored by Villeroy & Boch

a typical milk jug found in the store

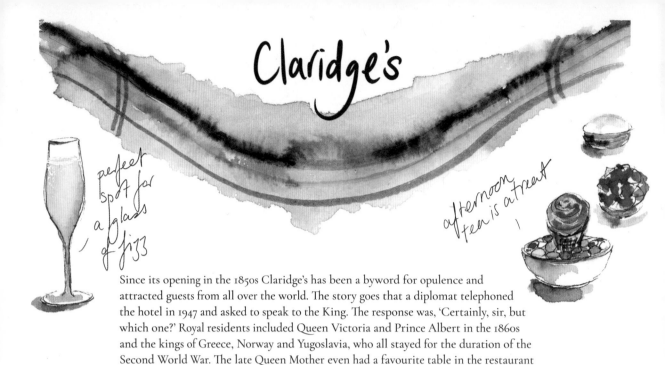

Claridge's

perfect spot for a glass of fizz

afternoon tea is a treat

Since its opening in the 1850s Claridge's has been a byword for opulence and attracted guests from all over the world. The story goes that a diplomat telephoned the hotel in 1947 and asked to speak to the King. The response was, 'Certainly, sir, but which one?' Royal residents included Queen Victoria and Prince Albert in the 1860s and the kings of Greece, Norway and Yugoslavia, who all stayed for the duration of the Second World War. The late Queen Mother even had a favourite table in the restaurant that was always adorned with sweet peas.

The hotel was redesigned between the wars and many of the Art Deco features from that time remain today. Step through the revolving doors into the magnificent lobby with its monochrome geometric tiled floor and you are transported to another world. This Mayfair institution is still the place for bon vivants to have fun. It serves over 60,000 bottles of Champagne a year and film stars, models, artists, fashionistas and musicians flock here.

I love the foyer and reading room, which has flowers to die for, and under the majestic Chihuly chandelier and Art Deco mirrors, it's a perfect spot to have afternoon tea or lunch. The Christmas tree positioned by the sweeping staircase in the lobby tops it all for me, it's a Claridge's tradition and something I always watch out for. Every year the tree is created by an artist, designer or fashion house, whose creative concoctions delight and amaze us. Sandra Choi for Jimmy Choo made a tower tree topped with a pink neon bow in 2022, and previous years can be seen below. A treat of a visit every time.

designer trees at Christmas

Jimmy Choo

Kim Jones Dior

McQueens Flowers

Christian Louboutin

Nour El Nil

slow travel in style

Travel slowly and in style aboard Adelaide, one of Nour El Nil's dreamy Egyptian *dahabiyas* (boats), which take you on an unforgettable journey of a lifetime on the Nile. With trips running from Esna near Luxor to Aswan, they pride themselves on authenticity, tradition and charm. As you sip the renowned hibiscus tea you must adjust to the pace here, lounge on the striped sofas with chandeliers overhead, sit back and lose yourself in six days of utter relaxation.

hibiscus tea served on brass trays

The *dahabiyas* are small enough to pause en route at less crowded and more interesting places that larger cruise ships can't access. Each day brings new excitement as you disembark to visit Egyptian treasures from temples to textile markets, tombs to sandstone quarries, stopping for riverbank picnics and a sunset dip if you wish.

The interiors are what first caught my attention – each boat has its own distinct style with signature striped cushions, comfy wicker chairs and brass fittings. Bedrooms are identified by a coloured ribbon rather than a number, they have fresh white Egyptian cotton sheets of course and romantic mosquito nets, with blankets and shawls to protect you from the cool evening breeze. Every detail has been considered down to pretty marble pots of hibiscus flowers on tables.

Dining is communal, when you will quickly get to know other guests around long tables with fresh produce and the catch of the day as well as Egyptian delights such as fig jam and falafel (not together, though). Later, relax on one of the decks, immerse yourself a game of backgammon or laze in a hammock with a good book, glancing up every now and again to just take in that view. This is bucket-list travel at its best.

hibiscus flowers prettify the tables on board

Hacienda de San Rafael

Last summer we took the children on their first 'sort of' backpacking trip, interrailing through Europe. I say sort of because it did involve backpacks and trains, but not the kind of hostel stays you associate with backpacking. My husband booked this place (he said a big 'no' to hostels) and we rocked up, slightly dishevelled, wishing we were better dressed. This 18th-century gem, set in a former olive estate, is a relaxed family-run affair that has been restored organically and with great care. Our homely thatched-roof *casita* (a suite), where the children slept in the eaves, was bright and airy with rustic wooden touches and a hint of Andalusia. Lebrillo bowls, Spanish plates, the seagrass ceiling and big fans instantly transported us to holiday mode.

the chorus of the birds fills the air

There is a different frequency of pace here, gentle, with a delightful chilled vibe. It's a conscious decision by the wonderful Anthony, the owner, and it forces guests to slow down and switch the tech off, talk, read, hang out and appreciate life.

Breakfast is served al fresco under a private pergola with whitewashed seats and block-printed cushions and cloths. The décor has been sourced from all over the world: trays from Indonesia, handmade cushions, the perfect mugs for tea. A chorus of birds serenades you as vast trays arrive with home-baked goods, homemade jams and overflowing bowls of fruit and yoghurt. It's a feast to set anyone up for the day ahead. The hacienda is also a great spot for touring the Andalusian countryside, and a super day trip is to take off to the 'white villages' of Córdoba, Ronda and Grazalema.

Gentle evenings are spent watching the sunset over breathtaking views, followed by dinner in the dining room. At first glance it feels formal, but everyone has the same delicious meal, just as if you are a guest in someone's home. The final hours of the day are spent huddled around a large communal firepit sipping gin and tonics with the smoky scent of *Bougainvillea* and easy chats with other guests from far and wide. I very much hope to be back there again soon.

cushions with their branding iron logo

huge vases of cotton bolls are displayed in rooms

Osborne House

Queen Victoria loved to play cards after dinner

I had to include one of Queen Victoria's favourite residences in the book as it is one of the loveliest places to visit on the Isle of Wight. Built as a family home by the sea, the house embodies Victorian family values. Its Italianate design became known as the Osborne style and many households of the time emulated the interiors and palettes used. It is dear to my heart, too, as my ancestor Edward Henry Corbould, also a watercolourist, spent much time here as art tutor (Instructor of Historical Painting no less) to Queen Victoria's children. Much of his work was purchased by the Queen and Prince Albert and we still have in our family the many black-edged letters he wrote to his wife and children from Osborne.

Drawing room

The drawing room at Osborne is filled with Corinthian marble columns, scrolling acanthus leaves and gold and yellow, giving a truly regal and opulent feel. This palette was reserved only for the royals or aristocrats of the time. It's hard to believe that colours such as yellow would not usually be seen in more modest Victorian households such as Sambourne (page 164). The yellow damask satin curtains and upholstery that you see today were restored using archive samples in 2003 and the carpet is a replica of the original Aubusson design. The Queen loved this space and often retired here after dinner to play cards. In the council room, which has a silk chenille carpet that was exhibited at the Great Exhibition, Alexander Graham Bell demonstrated his new invention, the telephone, in 1878.

Corinthian ornate marble columns with scrolling acanthus

letter from EH Corbould from his time at Osborne

detail of colourful cornice

Durbar room

The Durbar room was designed by Rudyard Kipling's father, Lockwood Kipling and Indian master carver Bhai Ram Singh as an entertaining space for banquets and receptions. The Queen was given the title Empress of India by Benjamin Disraeli and was fascinated by Indian culture, although she never visited the country. She completed this room after Prince Albert's death and it contains exquisite examples of intricate Indian plasterwork, Indian chintz and embossed wallpaper. The plasterwork centrepiece, a peacock, sits proudly over the teak fireplace and took over 500 hours to complete. This was also the first room in the house to be lit with electricity, and at Christmas a tree that almost reached the ceiling would be displayed with presents all around – quite a sight to behold.

the ceiling of the Durbar room is equally ornate

Swiss cottage

One of the best spots to explore at Osborne is the Swiss cottage. Tucked away from the main house, this Alpine-style chalet was built for the children and has its own gardens and even a museum. This was the royal children's own private place, where they learned about the wider world. Victorians enjoyed showcasing their curiosities and travel finds in glass cases and the children collected all manner of things from specimens found on the beach and insects and fossils, to the first ever transatlantic telegraph message. The museum even includes a rather odd stuffed deer with five legs! At the cottage, the children were taught to cook and keep house and most probably my ancestor taught some of their art lessons here, too. Everything was built at three-quarter size to make it child-friendly and it even had its very own dairy room where they learned to make cheese. Each child had their own garden plot, too, and their own wheelbarrows, tools and watering cans – which were monogrammed with their initials to avoid any squabbles.

Today you can walk through the trees to the beach and enjoy an ice-cream, view Queen Victoria's bathing hut and in the summer months take in the delights of the traditional Punch and Judy show (which my children adored when they were little).

Queen Victoria's bathing hut

the Punch & Judy is well worth a watch

– icecreams are a must

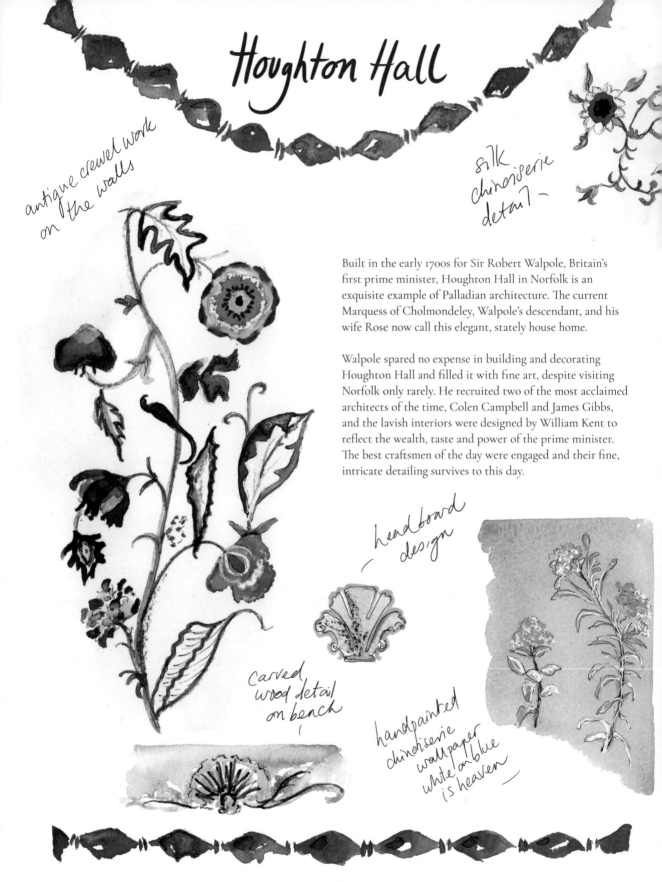

Houghton Hall

antique crewel work on the walls

silk chinoiserie detail —

Built in the early 1700s for Sir Robert Walpole, Britain's first prime minister, Houghton Hall in Norfolk is an exquisite example of Palladian architecture. The current Marquess of Cholmondeley, Walpole's descendant, and his wife Rose now call this elegant, stately house home.

Walpole spared no expense in building and decorating Houghton Hall and filled it with fine art, despite visiting Norfolk only rarely. He recruited two of the most acclaimed architects of the time, Colen Campbell and James Gibbs, and the lavish interiors were designed by William Kent to reflect the wealth, taste and power of the prime minister. The best craftsmen of the day were engaged and their fine, intricate detailing survives to this day.

headboard design

carved wood detail on bench

handpainted chinoiserie wallpaper white on blue is heaven —

shell bed by William Kent featured in the State rooms

don't forget to look up, the ceilings are incredible

The imposing mansion follows Palladian rules of symmetry, proportion and perspective inspired by Roman and Greek architecture, and the Cholmondeleys have ensured that lovers of modern art will find plenty of interest here, too. Eminent artists' work can be enjoyed inside and out, in the walled gardens and extensive parkland inhabited by white fallow deer. Damien Hirst, Henry Moore, Anish Kapoor and Tony Cragg are just a few who have exhibited here, and many pieces grace the walls and lawns permanently.

I was introduced to Houghton Hall when I spotted the *Cabana* magazine collaboration of table linen, china and glassware inspired by artefacts from the house, including antique silk that adorns Lady Rose's bedroom. It's a heavenly collaboration, from silk lace coasters to regal blue and terracotta floral dinnerware – a chance to have a piece of Houghton in your own home.

The bedroom shown on page 129 features antique crewelwork walls and a sublime fuchsia-pink quilted silk bedspread that bears the Marquess's grandmother's cipher. This is just a peek into the bedroom – you will have to visit to see the rest!

A Paris chez Antoinette Poisson

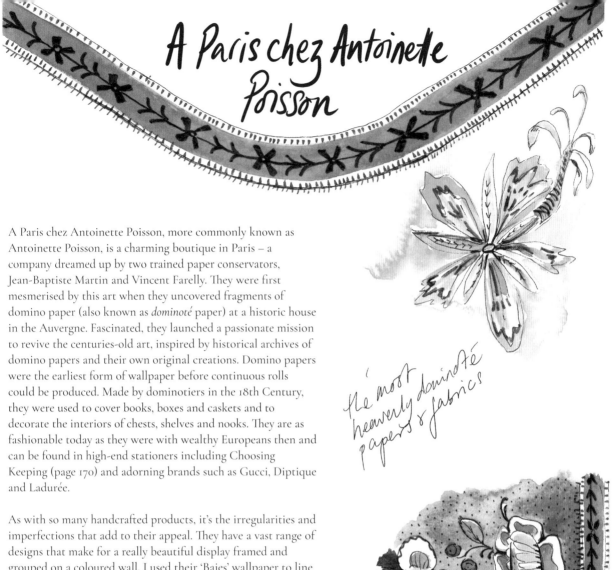

A Paris chez Antoinette Poisson, more commonly known as Antoinette Poisson, is a charming boutique in Paris – a company dreamed up by two trained paper conservators, Jean-Baptiste Martin and Vincent Farelly. They were first mesmerised by this art when they uncovered fragments of domino paper (also known as *dominoté* paper) at a historic house in the Auvergne. Fascinated, they launched a passionate mission to revive the centuries-old art, inspired by historical archives of domino papers and their own original creations. Domino papers were the earliest form of wallpaper before continuous rolls could be produced. Made by dominotiers in the 18th Century, they were used to cover books, boxes and caskets and to decorate the interiors of chests, shelves and nooks. They are as fashionable today as they were with wealthy Europeans then and can be found in high-end stationers including Choosing Keeping (page 170) and adorning brands such as Gucci, Diptique and Ladurée.

As with so many handcrafted products, it's the irregularities and imperfections that add to their appeal. They have a vast range of designs that make for a really beautiful display framed and grouped on a coloured wall. I used their 'Baies' wallpaper to line my own kitchen shelves and drawers at home and it truly adds a touch of French happiness to otherwise uninteresting spaces.

the most heavenly dominoté papers & fabrics

papers are printed & coloured by hand

the palettes used are soft and dusty

Parker Palm Springs

be sure to visit the lemonade stand to cool off

I visited this design-led hotel for my 30th birthday when we lived in California, and have the fondest of memories of my time here. I remember being greeted at the breeze-block entrance by the iconic burnt orange door (there is no sign outside) and feeling slightly embarrassed by our small (by American standards) and rather clapped-out car. Inside the entrance, all embarrassment was quickly forgotten as I was blown away by the edgy mid-century vibe with lots of coloured glass, and it still has the same hedonistic air. Set in 13 acres, it was formerly California's first Holiday Inn, then home to Gene Autry's baseball team, and today it is part of Merv Griffin's holdings. Interior design is by Jonathan Adler, and how it looks today is Adler's reimagined version from 2017. The décor is slightly crazy in a great way – very rock and roll – and kitsch at its best. This hip place oozes with characterful punchy colours and playful elements such as the two-metre bronze banana on the lawn. It is the place to be in Palm Springs.

The colourful poolside lemonade stand with yellow-and-white striped awning is shown opposite. It's the perfect spot to cool off after games on the lawn or a hammock snooze. There is a surprise around every corner, with the huge indoor firepit – a super place to take away the night-time desert chill and hang out for the evening. The restaurants are exceptional – I can still taste the chicken I had at Mister Parker's. The grounds are as lush as the interiors with overgrown grasses and citrus trees and, of course, over 200 palm trees. It really is the ultimate desert escape.

coloured glass display in every shape & hue

Treehouse Trancoso

This holiday home and tree house guest space can be found on the Discovery Coast of laidback Bahia in Brazil with UNESCO-protected shores and backed by thick jungle it feels like an unspoiled paradise.

Trancoso is a seriously hip place to holiday and, drawn by the natural beauty, historic charm and bohemian vibe, celebrity designers Robert and Cortney Novogratz have created a stunning retreat in this small fishing village. It's a simple and luxurious space, very casual, open-plan and full of fun design details. Kick off your shoes at the door because this is a seriously barefoot kind of space. Indigenous and reclaimed materials (eucalyptus, tatajuba and paraju trees) and local craftsmen's skills have been key to creating the authentic, slightly rustic Bahia look. Nothing shiny and slick but a fun, airy, relaxed getaway full of the bohemian aesthetic the Novogratz are known for.

Brazilian flag artwork

greenery all around

charming painted furniture & unique finds are dotted around the house

rustic natural lamps at a relaxed feel

There are wonderful spaces to make memories and gather, from the enormous hand-carved dining table to the shaded outdoor bar complete with 7-foot clay pizza oven (shown here). Or perhaps retreat for a siesta in the canopied bed in the treehouse, nestled up high with a view to die for and the romance of a mosquito net dancing in the breeze. Multiple doors open out from the living area on to an expansive veranda, large lampshades swinging overhead. The natural wooden structure is a wonderful warm canvas, highlighted by dashes of colour everywhere from the lush, tropical plants to the fuchsia-pink and pea-green bathrooms, cobalt cupboards, green ping pong table, and bold artwork like the embroidered Brazilian flag (shown above) – the Novogratz touch is sublime.

Victoria & Albert Museum

view looking up at the columns

On almost every trip to London I try to zip into the V&A to explore its maze of corridors lined with artefacts. This world-class collection of visual arts and design is constantly evolving, and I delight in something new each time I visit. I am instantly calmed by the cool marble floors, and rooms where there is always a quiet spot to marvel alone. Queen Victoria laid the first foundation stone in 1899 and today the collection numbers close to three million objects.

The buildings that make up the V&A are the finest examples of Victorian architecture and a trip to the café, made up of three rooms and featured here, is a must. When it opened in 1868 it was described as 'the world's first museum restaurant'. The Gamble Room is a feast for the eyes with colourful English tin-glazed majolica-tiled columns by painter Godfrey Sykes, who was responsible for much of the interior until his untimely death, when the baton was passed to designer James Gamble. Gamble's embellishments included ceramic ornamentation from cherubs and cupids to carved elephants and camels around the door frames. The space was designed with practicalities in mind – tiled surfaces were easy to clean, posed no fire risk and didn't attract food odours.

The Poynter Room (designed by Edward Poynter) was a showcase for the Aesthetic movement, and heavily influenced by Eastern designs, with floral and peacock motifs in Dutch blue paint. The tiles were made by female students who attended a porcelain class at the National Art Training School; it was most unusual for women to be commissioned for such a project at the time.

fire surround detail

giant vase in café

The Morris Room, (you guessed it) designed by William Morris, is the third space you can visit for a lunch break. Morris was only 31 when he designed this space, also known as the Green Room. He roped in his friends Edward Burne-Jones and architect Philip Webb and together they adorned the space with friezes of hounds and hares and stained-glass windows to marvel at. The plasterwork olive-bough walls are an early example of the type of pattern Morris is so famous for. The Green Room was the place to go for artists of the time, and I wonder if my artist ancestor Edward Corbould, who was art tutor to Queen Victoria's children (page 125), also sipped from porcelain cups here. I was thrilled recently to find one of his paintings displayed in the V&A's British galleries.

One of my favourite areas of the museum is the ceramic displays on the fourth level. My mother was an antique ceramic restorer, and I grew up with the comforting, familiar patterns of chintzware and Wemyss Ware pottery. I am a collector myself now, mainly chipped, cast-aside objects from larger sets, but every one a little piece of treasure. Showstoppers housed here include Dutch Delftware, Chinese White Ware, and my favourite wine-glass coolers in every shape and size.

The textile collections never fail to inspire me, with over 75,000 objects from pre-dynastic Egypt to the present. I have fond memories of visiting the V&A archives and pulling out wooden boxes with treasures inside, from antique bedspreads, embroidered caskets and needlepoint cushions to all types of clothing. Having completed a textiles degree, I am still obsessed by anything to do with yarn. The intricacy and the hours of work in every item on display is astounding. I could pore over the old dye recipe books and colour charts for days.

The kimono collection enthrals me every time, featuring items from the 1600s onwards, always closed left over right and fastened securely with an obi sash. The classic shape has remained constant and the colours, patterns and motifs allowed the wearer to express themselves and their status in society. I want to take each one home with me! I have only begun to scratch the surface of the delights of the V&A and if you visit one place after reading this book, make this number one on your list.

Dòhachi teapot dated 1825

detail of fireplace tiles

Chintz young woman's cap

cinoline 1860-1865 sprung steel frame covered in wool & linen

silk crepe kimono fabric

Spiro Store

a maximalists dream —

Like a jewellery box on a bustling corner in New Farm, Queensland, Anna Spiro's store looks right at home with its pale pink Art Deco façade. In the early autumn months the jacaranda trees that line the nearby streets are at their spectacular violet best and prepare you for the rainbow of joy awaiting inside.

Anna is one of Australia's best-known interior designers, celebrated for her colourful aesthetic. For projects such as Halcyon Hotel (page 70) she regularly puts together carefully chosen items layered with bold and vibrant, patterned prints. She always gets the mix just right.

Her store is an Aladdin's cave of wonderful objects to give your own home a touch of Spiro magic. Anna's interior design studio is in the basement but the action is upstairs, which is overflowing with fabrics, homewares, antiques, art, furniture and even vintage clothes, all of which you can imagine in Anna's own home. The store is laid out as if you have entered a domestic space showcasing all these disparate wares, rather than in conventional shop style. There is nothing minimalist or quiet about this place. A cacophony of bright, interesting things assaults your senses but in a joyful, thoughtfully curated, inspiring way. Bold painted shelves display antique meat platters and gingham plate designs. Every few months the window display box is redecorated, inviting people to come in and explore again and again. It's hard to leave here without making even the smallest colourful purchase for your home.

Vast collections of plates & ceramics

the store has a mix of unique pieces & antique finds)

142

Deetjen's Big Sur Inn

cute details add character

If you are ever taking a road trip on the west coast of California and fancy a truly authentic stay, Deetjen's in Big Sur is an absolute must. I visited Deetjen's when I lived in California in the early 2000s, and if rustic charm is what you long for it doesn't get better than this.

The inn was built in the early 1930s by Helmuth and Helen Haight Deetjen, who lived in a tent alongside the Castro Canyon Creek while they gradually built up the group of rustic Norwegian-style buildings that you see today, in what is now known as the 'Big Sur' style of building. The redwood barn was constructed with reclaimed materials found on Cannery Row in Monterey, and it soon became the restaurant of choice for travellers wanting to experience the good life.

The rooms each have their own distinct identity. They brim with treasures and antiques, offering a glimpse of the past and a whiff of intrigue. Names such as Van Gogh (a nod to the painter's bedroom in Arles), Edy's and Faraway, and their quaint descriptions such as 'small and sweet, nestled behind the canopy of the magnolia' lure repeat guests back time and time again. You can even stay in 'Grandpa's' (Helmuth's) own room, with his prized vinyl collection to enjoy. One thing is guaranteed – there is no internet, phone or mobile signal here. Rooms contain journals to which guests can add their own special memories, and it's hard not to stay up all night flicking through the pages. The beating heart of Deetjen's Inn, however, is the restaurant, where you can enjoy the simple pleasure of dinner by candlelight warmed by fires and wine. This place certainly warms the soul.

toasty blankets to snuggle under

journals in every room for guests to share their best bits & stories of their stay

tables are candlelit creating a cosy vibe

Bar Palladio

Dreamed up by Swiss–Italian owner Barbara Miolini, and with interiors by Dutch designer Marie-Anne Oudejans, the Bar Palladio restaurant in Jaipur is an interior lover's dream. Miolini was formerly with the Cipriani in Venice (page 49) before moving to Jaipur to set up an embroidery factory. She decided to open a European-style café, much like Caffè Florian (page 109), and so Bar Palladio was born. This is no café in the traditional sense but, exquisitely, much, much more. Located in a restored garden in the historic Hotel Narain Niwas Palace, Bar Palladio presents Italian cuisine in an atmospheric and magical setting among mango trees and resident peacocks. The interior provides a backdrop with striking contrasts of bright cobalts against white. Every detail here has been created by local artisans, and it's a feast for all the senses. Bold colour at every corner in every shade of blue imaginable has been used to create a space to sit back and relax. Pillows are piled high on banquette seating and it's the perfect spot to admire the hand-carved panels and locally block-printed textiles, which add a charming, homely feel. This is a place to unwind and enjoy the simple pleasures of life.

brass lanterns cast a gentle light

every element & item has been selected to bring joy

striking monochrome palette of blue & white

Villa Palladio

floral motifs & zigzags galore

stripey bolster cushions to lean up against

tents for shade from the afternoon sun

The delightful Villa Palladio hotel opened in September 2022, located on an old silk road and only 20 minutes from the pink city of Jaipur. It is a place that transports you with vibrant décor and heaps of charm. This hotel is much like Bar Palladio in terms of decoration but instead of a theme of blue tones it is infused with scarlet and crimson reds. It's an intimate retreat with just nine rooms, each lovingly hand painted with green and white palm-leaf motifs against walls in strong pinks and reds. Candy-striped corridors lead to luxurious rooms with scallop-edged canopy beds and geometric black and white floor tiles. The effect is stunning; this is a jewel of a place, packing a punch at every turn. Each surface is filled with pattern from red and white stripes to floral motifs – they haven't missed an inch – and the colour continues outside with an impressive arched pool house with red-and-white zigzags on the columns and the same stripes on the loungers. There is a spa to enjoy, a library to discover and gardens of jasmine and native plants to explore, too.

Miolini and Oudejans have the magic touch; they have invigorated the colours of the place with an energy and vibrancy that is unrivalled. I cannot wait to find out what is next for this duo and what hues they choose for future ventures together.

every inch of the place is covered in pattern & colour

The Whitby Hotel

Kit's collection of baskets is exquisite

I arrived at the Whitby in Midtown Manhattan straight off the plane and in a blur after the launch of my first book. I was treated to the most wonderful tour of every nook and cranny of this stunning hotel, just two blocks from Central Park. The lobby greets you with playful colour and wit, blending together craft from Hermione Skye's loom (whose work also features in the lobby of the Ham Yard Hotel, page 182) with art installations such as the grandfather clock by Maarten Baas, with a graphic animation of the grandfather inside the clock, rewriting with a felt-tip pen every minute of time passing. Next, you come to the drawing room, an intimate space for drinks where the honesty bar is a nice touch, ensuring you don't have to wait to top up!

Hermione Sky's loom artwork in the lobby

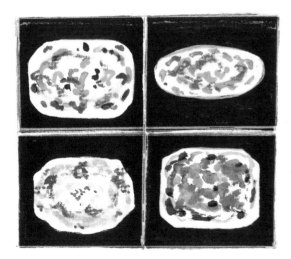

The rooms are generous by New York standards with all the iconic elements of a Firmdale hotel. Oversized headboard – check, mannequin – check, comfy chairs and considered palettes and trim – check. I saw ten different rooms, amazed by how designer and hotelier Kit Kemp and her team pull it together.

The star attraction for me was Kit's collection of baskets. Above the bar is a vast installation of every shape and weave imaginable. Anyone who knows me well knows I have a basket for every occasion and can rarely resist a purchase. Kit clearly has the same obsession and has collected and tagged every one that hangs over the bar documenting when and where she found it ... basket heaven!

Antique plates in perspex boxes make a stunning wall display

Petersham Nurseries

wisteria vines add magic

Petersham elephant logo

This is one of those destinations you simply must visit for an enjoyable day out with friends. Gael and Francesco Boglione created the family institution that is Petersham Nurseries and since opening the doors in 2004 they haven't looked back. They started with the tranquil nursery and, once complete with café, it became a space where people could amble around, browse plants and homewares, and enjoy tea and cake. Over time, it's evolved into today's honest mix of wholesome foods, special finds from India and Indonesia, as well as antique treasures and treats. It's an effortless mix of zinc-topped tables, stone statues, vintage bud vases and Murano glass. Oh, and don't forget the flowers – every dreamy type you can imagine. The Bogliones' daughters Lara, the Managing Director, and buyer Ruby ensure that every item suits the relaxed, easy aesthetic that is synonymous with the brand. If ever there was organic growth this is it, it feels as if everything happened naturally, from a casual chat with Skye Gyngell about maybe adding a tea shop to the business, to starting with a simple table for ten in the middle of the greenhouse to a thriving, award-winning restaurant, which now holds a coveted green Michelin star. Lara's travels inspire the homeware collections, too, and Francesco's love of coloured glass is evident in the vast array on offer here. This is truly a place to unwind under the pergola of wisteria and *Bougainvillea*, starlit with fairy lights in the evening, and enjoy local produce and home-cooked pleasures. It is pure magic.

bud vases of flowers on every table

coloured glass vessels in every shade & design

rustic pots

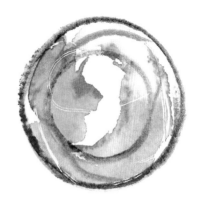

Extending the successful brand further, they took the country to central London. Smack bang in the middle of Covent Garden is an oasis of calm with the Petersham Deli, La Goccia Restaurant and Bar, plus acclaimed eatery The Petersham. The Petersham draws its style from the family home in Richmond; it is understated and refined but not stuffy, with the same rustic touches that are found at the nurseries. Taking the 'slow food' movement by storm, from plot to plate, they source ingredients from their own Haye Farm in Devon, run by son Harry. The Bar is the perfect spot for seasonal cocktails and the sweeping bar is made entirely of real leaves cast in bronze, a nod to its horticultural heritage. Oisín Byrne paintings of cheerful tulips add to the look (I spotted these immediately as I have an artist's proof of one of his screenprints, which I adore). La Goccia restaurant offers Italian fare, with the dishes prepared in full view of guests, creating a fun and dramatic (organic only) evening out.

bud vases in every size & shape

marbled plates

leaves cast in bronze make up the bar

hanging dried flowers add rustic charm

The Bogliones really care about the impact of their business on the environment. Uniforms are made from recycled bottles, waste turned into biofuels, wine corks recycled, packaging is 100% biodegradable ... you get the picture. The elephants that feature in their logo aren't forgotten either, with regular events supporting their favourite Elephant Family charity: you can feel good about any purchase here.

I love to while away hours in the Deli at Covent Garden. It's great for people-watching, and the seasonal salads and Italian *arancini* (rice balls) are definitely not to be missed. The interior is homely with fluted sinks, salt-glazed pots and dried flowers hanging from brass rails. I never want to leave.

delightful outdoor seating at zinc topped tables

Rosewood Luang Prabang

on stilts high above the forest floor

Nestled in the verdant jungle of northern Laos, luxury tented accommodation is the setting for a real treat of a stay. Rosewood is located near Luang Prabang, a UNESCO World Heritage Site, yet set apart in rainforest along the steep banks of the Mekong River. Surrounded by streams and natural waterfalls, it is a heavenly hideaway. Each tent features a bedroom for two, its own dining area and a 360-degree deck where you can invite guests to take in every inch of the breathtaking views.

Chapans in frames can be found on the bedroom walls

references to ancient temples are reflected in the decor

Each tent (there are also villas) has its own spirit of adventure, with designer Bill Bensley pulling together elements of the local heritage with his own bold colour choices and zest. The décor is also inspired by the French–Laotian architecture for which Luang Prabang is known. There is a romance to it all, with dark mahogany woods, crisp bed linen and artefacts sourced from Parisian flea-market buying trips. Chapans (traditional long coats) are framed on the walls alongside artwork by the area's indigenous people.

There is plenty to explore outside, too, in the gardens created by Bensley with an abundant supply of fruits, vegetables, blooms and other plant species that have long fascinated visitors to this special part of the world.

The Square & Compass

Having holidayed for years on the Isle of Purbeck in Dorset, I first stumbled upon this pub in Worth Matravers by accident when looking for a spot for lunch with a walk and a view. The first nice touch is the honesty car park; how wonderful is that – it sets the right tone. And as pubs go, it doesn't get better than this one. The view is the first thing that mesmerises you, as you're high up on the cliffs overlooking fields to the sea. Each season here brings new joy, even winter's blustery walks and bracing winds, bendy, battered trees and the white horses bobbing on the horizon.

In the winter months the pub offers a welcome retreat, with large open fires and shared tables where you are sure to make new friends. They keep things simple, only serving pies and pasties (one veggie and one meat option) on paper plates with local beer. In summer, big blue skies are flecked with seabirds, and we sit outside with pints at the monumental stone tables, joined by hens pecking around our feet and lots of doggie friends. The pub even has its own museum, a collector's dream of Jurassic Coast finds, including giant crabs and even a crocodile – its contents wow visitors great and small.

After that first visit, I phoned my mother with excitement to tell her that I'd truly found the best pub in the whole wide world and she promptly replied, 'You have found the Square and Compass then, it was your grandparents' favourite pub, too.' She sent me a photo of herself and my uncles sitting outside as children and I love it even more knowing that it was always their number one, too.

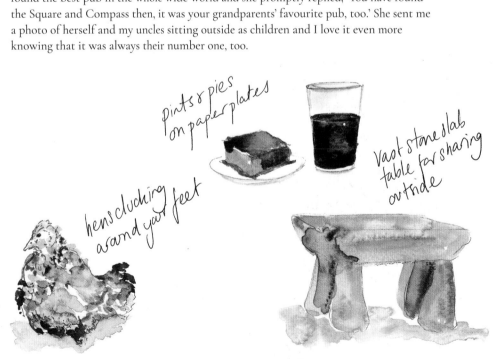

pints & pies on paper plates

hens clucking around your feet

Vast stone slab table for sharing outside

The Connaught Bar

Regularly voted one of the best bars in the world, the Connaught Bar is the best place to sip a martini, especially if it comes from the bespoke drinks trolley. My favourite spot is in the window; you feel a little bit on display to the world, but it's a great place to people-watch – although all the drama is to be found inside.

This place just works – it is classic yet current, traditional yet innovative. The décor by David Collins Studio is refined and elegant with a modern twist. Cubist-inspired wood panelling dominates, with vast mirrors and the palest tint of green ceiling hinting at its early 19th-century origins. The lighting is intimate and the walls are textured in platinum silver leaf. Warm dark woods contrast with stark marble, and the green leather seating adds a touch of charm. Flair is the name of the game here; cocktails are served with panache, with innovative concoctions created by the world-renowned team of mixologists. The service, ceremony and theatre of it all makes this bar so much more than just somewhere to have a drink. With names like Wayfarer, Magnetum and Eclipse, the cocktails delve deep and feed your soul. There is even a house gin, with hints of juniper and Amalfi lemon peel giving it an extra flourish. The good news is you don't have to travel to London to try it, you can buy a bottle online and enjoy it at home, too!

THE place to sample a martini in London

juniper berry garnish,

famous martini trolley

Sambourne House

frilly lampshades

This is the former family home of illustrator Edward Linley Sambourne (known as Linley Sambourne), most famous for his work for *Punch* magazine and Charles Kingsley's *The Water Babies*. The house is one of the finest examples of the Aesthetic style and is preserved much as Sambourne left it. A stone's throw from Leighton House (page 98), this more modest home was equally loved and cherished and Sambourne spent years decorating it with William Morris and Lincrusta wallpapers, and adding many new features, including the impressive stained-glass window on the stair landing. The parquet flooring varies throughout, from basketweave to herringbone, while ceilings received the same treatment as the walls, almost cocooning you in the busy wallpaper designs. Cornices are ornate with scrolling ivy leaves and carved flowers, and high shelves beneath to display delicate Oriental plates and vases. Every corner of this place has been carefully decorated.

Today, you can wander around and imagine what it would have been like to live here in the 19th Century. The interior is very dark and there is a density and heavy feel to the house, as if it is creaking under the weight of the furniture and the sheer volume of contents. Almost every surface is covered in precious objects, from ceramics and clocks to hundreds of pictures.

everything they owned was on display

Morris Co wallpaper is featured here

Sambane has over 50 vases, 70 chairs & 700 framed pictures

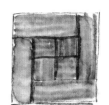

flooring designs from basket weave to parquet

The morning room is featured here, with William Morris wallpaper and a hand-painted door with stylised flowers. Note the heavy velvet curtain with its own pole on the door to keep out the draughts, far grander than you would expect for such an unassuming room. Even the fireplace has its own embellishments with a studded pelmet in dark velvet and pink tassel trimmings.

pretty bowls with breaks & cracks

ornate cornice details - wow

even the fireplace has been embellished with tassels & trim

The house was decorated on a shoestring, with pieces cleverly acquired at auction. They were often replicas or chipped and restored, which no one noticed when they were displayed high up. Sambourne was very economical; cramming the walls with pictures meant that he could use smaller samples of wallpaper, and with every wall filled people wouldn't notice the details. The overall effect is maximalist and probably not one to emulate at home nowadays, but it is inspiring to visit and explore this real Victorian home.

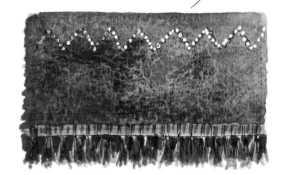

The Jane

This celebrated restaurant occupies a large, red-brick former chapel dating from 1911 in the Groen Kwartier (Green Quarter) of Antwerp. Originally part of a military hospital, the site stood empty for many years before renowned Dutch designer Piet Boon and master chef (and DJ!) Nick Bril renovated it, turning it into a culinary temple instead. Everything here is a work of art, from the building to the food, tablescapes and lighting.

The former altar houses the open kitchen behind a glazed screen where diners can witness the creation of their seasonal dishes. The Jane serves one tasting menu, comprised mainly of elegant seafood dishes, with Bril's food inspired by world flavours but with a strong focus on using produce from closer to home, especially the neighbouring rooftop garden. The space is grand and light, with classical bones and modern touches. Bril didn't want the place to feel rigid; it is welcoming and offers a clever mix of fine dining and exceptional service without the pomp and ceremony of formal restaurants.

The dramatic lighting installation overhead, with over 150 bulbs, covers 12 by 9 metres. Suspended from a single point, it's a real showstopper. It is contrasted with white walls and magnificent contemporary stained-glass windows featuring everything from chocolate bars and croissants to ice-cream cones, smiley faces and the CND symbol, adding a touch of humour to the atmosphere. The Jane is a gastronomic and design triumph; if you're lucky enough to visit Antwerp, put it at the top of your list.

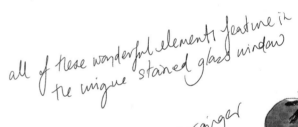

all of these wonderful elements feature in the unique stained glass window

paksoi & ginger cocktail

Choosing Keeping

Tucked away on the corner of Tower Street, just off Covent Garden's St Martin's Lane, is the dreamiest shop for artists and stationery lovers. The first thing you notice is the handmade wrought-iron sign, made by a master forger, depicting a Bavarian-style phoenix with an inkwell in its beak. It feels traditional and solid, and perfectly formed; a glimpse of what is inside.

This feels like a store that's been here forever. Old-fashioned cases house fountain pens and tall glass display cabinets showcase every paint pigment imaginable. Each item is carefully sourced by the team with the aim of keeping dying art-and-craft products alive. Only well made, high-quality items that haven't been mass-produced feature here. I cannot imagine a single person walking out of the store without making a purchase.

Nothing is ordinary, from the plethora of pens and pencils to sketchbooks, Japanese papers and every wrap you could wish for special gifts. My greatest loves include the realistic fruit-shaped wax candles, laser-cut postcards that look like lace, wet and dry pastels in stunning unusual hues, my trusty green Bakelite pencil sharpener, ceramic brush pots and the Japanese watercolour paints that I've used on this very page. Make a special visit to this London shop, it will be worth every second.

my favourite bakerlite sharpener

the paint set I curated

clementine shaped candles

brushes and pigments galore

Mochaware brush pots in seaweed design are a favourite

Villa Posillipo

a peek at the delightful interior

Whenever I'm longing for a bit of comfort and nostalgia I return to one of my all-time favourite TV series, The Durrells. Based on the book *My Family and Other Animals* by Gerald Durrell it is set in the beauty of the Ionian islands where the author lived. I was thrilled to learn that you can stay in the idyllic spot where much of the series was filmed – an 18th-century Venetian-style villa, 'Posillipo', on the east coast of Corfu (bookings via thethinkingtraveller.com). Perfectly secluded in an acre of gardens on the edge of the sea, it is just a stone's throw from The White House, the former residence of Gerald's brother Lawrence Durrell.

The light here is incredible, from the bright blue sky and sea to the whitewashed interiors, shaded hammock, dappled al-fresco dining spots and sun illuminating the house through the tall windows and doors. Indoors or outdoors, it is all beautiful here, with magnificent views. A wonderful stone terrace surrounds the villa. It drops directly to the sea on one side and is backed by lush gardens on the others. Crunch up the gravel path, past the palm, pine, fig and olive trees, then up the stairs to the green front door. High ceilings, the original tiled floor and an atmosphere of calm welcome you, while a grand piano hints at fun to be had. There's a well-curated mix of antique, local and modern furnishings.

enjoy fresh figs with yoghurt & honey for breakfast

famous green shutters

couldn't resist featuring a pelican here

Throw open the doors to feel the sea breeze, read on your lounger listening to the sea lapping against the wall, doze in the hammock taking in the fragrance of the Italian stone pines, pick fresh vegetables from the garden for lunch or gather freshly laid eggs from the resident hens for breakfast. Explore the night sky through the villa's own telescope, or venture through the secret gate to the shingle beach where the clearest of waters greets you. Every moment here is pure magic...

The Woodman's Hut

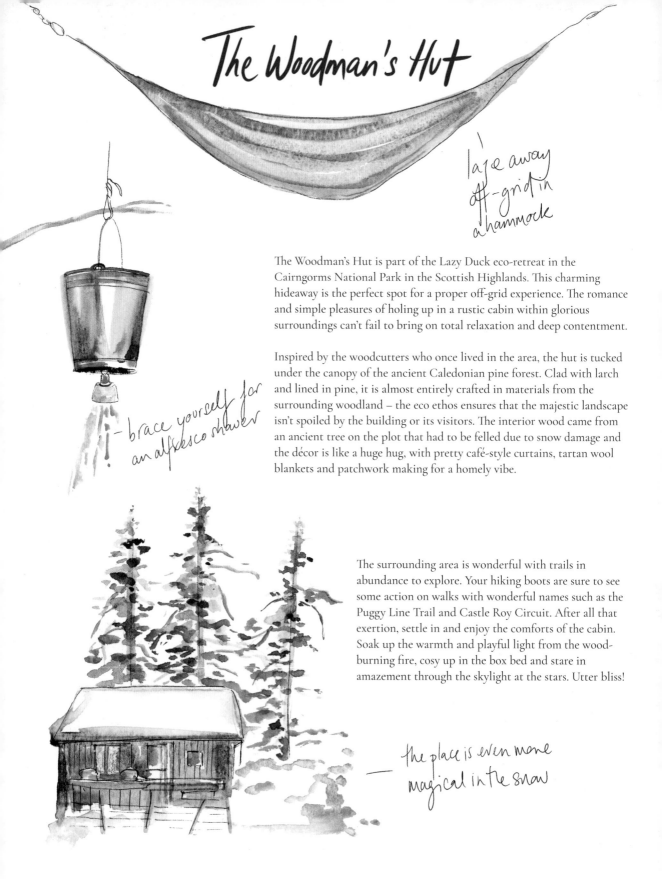

laze away off-grid in a hammock

— brace yourself for an alfkesco shower

The Woodman's Hut is part of the Lazy Duck eco-retreat in the Cairngorms National Park in the Scottish Highlands. This charming hideaway is the perfect spot for a proper off-grid experience. The romance and simple pleasures of holing up in a rustic cabin within glorious surroundings can't fail to bring on total relaxation and deep contentment.

Inspired by the woodcutters who once lived in the area, the hut is tucked under the canopy of the ancient Caledonian pine forest. Clad with larch and lined in pine, it is almost entirely crafted in materials from the surrounding woodland – the eco ethos ensures that the majestic landscape isn't spoiled by the building or its visitors. The interior wood came from an ancient tree on the plot that had to be felled due to snow damage and the décor is like a huge hug, with pretty café-style curtains, tartan wool blankets and patchwork making for a homely vibe.

The surrounding area is wonderful with trails in abundance to explore. Your hiking boots are sure to see some action on walks with wonderful names such as the Puggy Line Trail and Castle Roy Circuit. After all that exertion, settle in and enjoy the comforts of the cabin. Soak up the warmth and playful light from the wood-burning fire, cosy up in the box bed and stare in amazement through the skylight at the stars. Utter bliss!

— the place is even more magical in the snow

Shane Confectionery

sweet pie bon bon treats

milk chocolate seashells

Located in Philadelphia, this confectionery shop is brimming with tradition. It is one of the longest-running candy stores in the US, open since 1863. Shane Confectionery was part of a once-flourishing 19th-century scene when cocoa, fruits and spices were shipped up the Delaware River to satisfy customers' sweet-toothed desires. Sugar cane was refined locally and Philadelphia soon became the place to go for quality confectionery.

they even tried to grow their own cocoa beans!

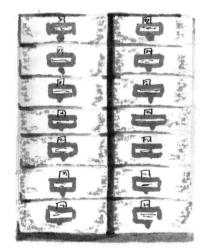

Besides all the sweeties, what caught my attention here was the vast bank of drawers in the back room. There are 220, resembling metal filing cabinets and containing over a thousand Victorian toy-shaped moulds. These are used to continue a tradition of producing 'clear toy' candy treats (coloured hard candy in intricate shapes) today. Each mould is categorised by number and type, so a drawer may read 'number 87 – animal pairs', 'number 88 – pigs' and so on. It's a wonderful collection of confectionery history.

Shane uses secret recipe books, worn and yellowed over time, for the 100-year-old buttercream recipe, which is still made on the same 100-year-old machine. They use local ingredients where possible and responsibly sourced cocoa beans, which are turned into Shane chocolate and made into bars, hot chocolate or ice cream. Every day sugar is boiled in copper kettles to create an ark of animals from the Victorian moulds. These are hand cooled on marble, embellished with the finest decoration, packaged and sent to adorn tables around the world. It has given me a new appreciation for the artistry of candy making.

orderly drawers contain antique chocolate moulds

nostalgic candy can be found here gobstopper/jaw breaker

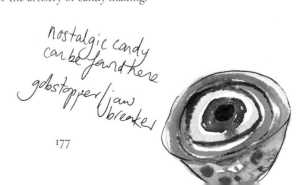

Pitt Rivers Museum

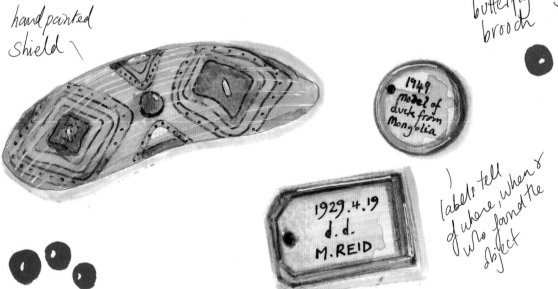

I adore the tradesmen's bead cards

604
608
606
607

1
2
3
4
8

In 1884, archaeologist General Pitt-Rivers gifted his collection to the University of Oxford, leading to the creation of a museum like no other. Every time I visit Oxford I have to stop by, even if it's for just half an hour. It houses the most incredible collections that are ordered by type, rather than by geographical region or date. This allows visitors to compare materials and corresponding traits across different cultures. Objects, whether kitchen utensils or musical instruments, come from every corner of the world and are housed in characteristically overcrowded cases. Intricate hand-written labels recording where, when and who found the object have been retained from the earliest days of the museum.

I find this museum a particularly inspiring resource for design, pattern and ideas. I cram sketchbooks full of drawings of pieces from colourful salesmen's beads to Persian embroidered cloths or a Hawaiian food-pounding stone. There are Arctic coats made of intestines, the tiniest beads made from stalactites, voice disguisers, voodoo dolls, textiles from every culture and craft, carved masks, figures and shields galore. With the most obscure and intriguing artefacts, you are sure to find something new to astound you on every visit.

butterfly wing brooch

hand painted shield

1949 model of duck from Mongolia

1929.4.19
d.d.
M. REID

labels tell of where, when & who found the object

The Exvotos

vases are decorated with flowers & feathers —

Run by Andalusian artists Luciano Galán and Daniel Maldonado, this is a Seville ceramic workshop where every piece celebrates Spain's artistic heritage. I first came across this pair in lockdown, when I painted vignettes of their coveted head vases filled with bunches of eucalyptus and carnations. Inspired by the idea of 'ex-voto' objects (votive offerings to gods or saints), the duo bring together sculpture and ceramics with humour and respect to create homewares from lamps and candlesticks to their much sought-after head vases. Religion, nature, theatre and history all play their part in making these pieces so special. Each is unique and tells a story. Made with organic materials in clay, wood, paper or cloth and using ancient techniques, they feel traditional but sit well in a modern environment. The head vases became iconic when they featured in TV series 'White Lotus' (page 18).

heart earring from head vase

Galán and Maldonado's studio is a work of art in itself, it can be found (by appointment only) tucked away in one of the many pastel-hued side streets. Every surface here seems to be hand painted and made with love, shelves are covered with painterly touches and they have their own signature candles whose name aptly translates as 'scent of holiness'. Deep shelves display stuffed birds and sculptures under Victorian glass cloches and paint-chipped furniture has been salvaged from another life. Hand-painted plates and platters, candlesticks and vases in every shape imaginable can be found here. The head vases are the showstoppers though, these dramatic, highly decorative vessels are heirloom pieces to be treasured by generations to come.

they always seem to have quite serious expressions

Ham Yard Hotel

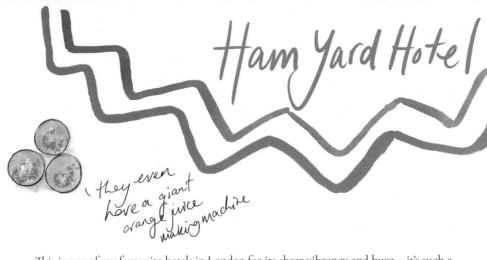

they even have a giant orange juice making machine

This is one of my favourite hotels in London for its sheer vibrancy and buzz – it's such a super place to hang out and enjoy. The name comes from an early 18th-century public house called The Ham that was once on the site. It's hard to imagine that this spot was bombed in the Blitz and left derelict for some time before Kit Kemp and her team came to the rescue. On arrival in the bustling courtyard you are greeted by a Tony Cragg bronze sculpture, Group. I adore Cragg's work and first fell in love with his opaque glass sculptures, featured at Tate Modern in the late 1990s. This is just a taste of the art to come, with installation after installation of joy to be found around every corner.

Walk through the lobby to the bar and on the way marvel at the swags of wicker light fittings in every colour imaginable. The long space is inspired by the Caribbean paintings that are set in wooden boxes at the bar, hand painted in delightful monochrome designs. At one end of the room Martha Freud pots are lit up inside, creating a wonderful glow that draws you in. You feel cocooned and comforted by the Christopher Farr lemon-yellow willow fabric that covers the walls. Journey on through glass doors to the orangery, where it's bright and breezy and feels a little quieter with wicker seating and a gentle palette of greens and neutrals.

astounding Tony Cragg sculpture in the entrance

woven lampshades make a spectacular display over the table

Rooms here are killer! With 91 to choose from, each with its own personality, they will always feature a dreamy signature oversized headboard in all manner of trims and finishes from embroidered to appliquéd, quilted to studded. Mannequins covered in fabrics add to the scheme and are associated with Kit's brilliant style. A Superior room is featured here, overlooking the leafy courtyard and London skyline. You won't want to leave.

Before you go, be sure to head to the little shop, open for hotel guests on request, where you can even find my interior portraits to take home as a memento.

The roof terrace

I first visited the large leafy terrace at an event to launch Kit Kemp's collection of rugs in collaboration with Annie Selke. A beautiful space on the fourth floor, it is a carefully maintained garden that even has bees, tended by a dedicated beekeeper. Their honey is used in the bar's extensive menu of cocktails. It's a wonderful place to sit under a canopy of spherical lightshades and enjoy this rare rooftop space in the centre of London's Soho.

lampshades hang elegantly from the canopy on the roof terrace

a favourite painting of a wedding bureau at the HXH.

The Croc bowling alley

Oh my goodness, where to start, it's an original 1950s solid maple bowling alley, imported from Texas. If that isn't enough, there is a wall lit up with row upon row of vintage bowling shoes in Perspex display cases, plus bowling-pin lamps and backlit balls. This is classic Kit Kemp design magic, where she creates a feature using unlikely objects, which looks incredible. The icing on the cake though are the two large Howard Hodgkin artworks – and don't forget the dancefloor and silver baby grand piano!

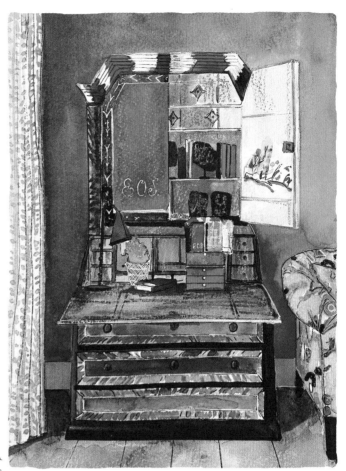

bowling alley shoes in perspex boxes make a fab display

☐ 25Hours Hotel Indre By
page 26

@25hourshotel_copenhagen

☐ A Paris chez Antoinette
Poisson   page 132

@antoinettepoisson

☐ Alchemist
page 28

@restaurantalchemist

☐ Babylonstoren
page 32

@babylonstoren

☐ Bar Palladio
page 146

@barpalladio

☐ British Pullman
page 36

@belmondbritishpullman

☐ Caffè Florian
page 109

@caffeflorian

☐ Cap Rocat
page 22

@cap_rocat

☐ Chandler House
page 90

@chandlerhousect

☐ Charleston
page 40

@charlestontrust

☐ Chatsworth House
page 14

@chatsworthofficial

☐ Choosing Keeping
page 170

@choosingkeeping

☐ Claridges
page 116

@claridgeshotel

☐ Claude Monet's House
page 82

@fondationmonet

☐ Cristine Bedfor
page 52

@cristinebedfor

☐ Daylesford Organic
page 56

@daylesfordfarm

☐ Deetjen's Big Sur Inn
page 144

@deetjensbigsurinn

☐ Dresdner Molkerei
Gebrüder Pfund   page 114

@pfunds_molkerei

☐ El Fenn
page 64

@elfennmarrakech

☐ GoldenEye, Ian Fleming
Villa   page 86

@goldeneye

☐ Gracy's
page 68

@gracysmalta

☐ Hacienda de San Rafael
page 122

@_halcyonhouse

☐ Halcyon House
page 70

@_halcyonhouse

☐ Ham Yard Hotel
page 182

@firmdale_hotels

☐ Hauser & Wirth
page 30

@hauserwirth

☐ Heckfield Place
page 79

@heckfield_place

☐ Horta Museum
page 92

@hortamuseum

☐ Hotel Cipriani
page 49

@belmondhotelciprian

☐ Hotel les Deux Gares
page 100

@hoteldeuxgares

☐ Houghton Hall
page 128

@houghton_hall

☐ HR Giger Bar Museum
page 80

@hr_giger_museum

☐ John Derian
page 76

@johnderiancompany

☐ La Mère de Famille
page 96

@alameredefamille

☐ Le Sirenuse
page 102

@lesirenuse

☐ Leighton House
page 98

@leightonsambournemuseums

☐ Liberty
page 110

@libertylondon

☐ Nour El Nil
page 118

@nourelnil

☐ Osborne House
page 124

@englishheritage

☐ Parker Palm Springs
page 134

@parkerpalmsprings

☐ Petersham Nurseries
page 152

@petershamnurseries

☐ **Pitt Rivers Museum**
page 178

@pittriversmuseum

☐ **Populart**
page 24

@populartsevilla

☐ **Rosewood Luang Prabang**
page 158

@rosewoodluangprabang

☐ **Salthrop House**
page 94

@sophieconran

☐ **Sambourne house**
page 164

@leightonandsambournemuseums

☐ **San Domenico**
page 18

@fstaormina

☐ **Shane Confectionery**
page 176

@shaneconfectionery

☐ **Shell Grotto**
page 46

@shellgrotto

☐ **Sketch**
page 72

@sketchlondon

☐ **Spiro Store**
page 142

@spiro.store

☐ **The Connaught Bar**
page 162

@theconnaught

☐ **The Exvotos**
page 180

@theexvotos

☐ **The Fife Arms**
page 61

@thefifearms

☐ **The Jane**
page 168

@thejaneantwerp

☐ **The Square and Compass**
page 160

@squareandcompasspub

☐ **The Whitby Hotel**
page 150

@lartisienofficial

☐ **The Woodman's Hut**
page 174

@thelazyduck

☐ **Treehouse Trancoso**
page 136

@thenovogratz

☐ **Ulysses**
page 88

@hotelulysses

☐ **Victoria and Albert Museum**
page 138

@vamuseum

☐ Villa Palladio
page 148
@villa.palladio.jaipur

☐ Villa Posillipo
page 172
@villaposillipo

☐ Wormsley Estate
page 34
@wormsleyestate

ABOUT THE AUTHOR

SJ Axelby was born in Wiltshire and is from a long lineage of artists, including the designer of the Penny Black Stamp and the art teacher to Queen Victoria's children. She captures interiors through watercolour and mixed media bringing rooms to life. She is host of @roomportraitclub where you too can join in and make your own interior portrait. She lives and works from her studio in Buckinghamshire, UK.

PHOTOGRAPHY CREDITS

Thank you to everyone that has made this book happen, to the people that shared special places with me and the photographers that allowed me to use their photographs as references for my paintings.

25hours Hotel Indre By – Martin Brudnizki

Chatworth – Antonio Monfredo

Cipriani (water scene) – Belmond/Betsi Ewig

Cipriani (room scene) – Belmond/Tyson Sadlo

Cipriani (window scene) – Belmond/Helen Cathcart

Cipriani (orange scene) – Belmond/Mary Quincy

Cipriani (cover) – Belmond/Marco Valmarana

Fife Arms – Sim Cannetty-Clarke/ *House and Garden*

Giger Bar – Andy Davies

Gracy's – Antoina Deeson

Hauser and Wirth Menorca – Daniel Schafer

Horta Museum – Brigita Soldo

Houghton Hall – Ashley Hicks

Leighton House – Anna Ambrosi

Osbourne House – Peter Shepherd

Osbourne House – Sarah Fortescue

San Domenico Palace – Four Seasons

Villa Palladio – Minnie Kemp

I've genuinely tried to credit all the wonderful photographers responsible for the images used to inspire the paintings in this book, if I have missed you off, I am very sorry, and please do get in touch so that we can make sure we credit you on any social-media use of the painting as well as any reprints.

thank you x

Thank you, thank you, thank you ... I still pinch myself that this is real. This book was so much harder to produce than the first and I had such big moments of self-doubt and many, many late nights that I couldn't have got through without the people mentioned here.

To Clare Double, Laura Russell and Stephanie Milner, plus Sian Baldwin, Caroline Oestergaard, Shamar Gunning, Lisa Milton, Hannah Naughton, Grace O'Byrne, Komal Patel, Lily Wilson and everyone at Pavilion and HarperCollins for believing in me and making this happen so wonderfully.

To all the wonderful places featured in this book, each and every one an honour and privilege to paint.

To the lovely people I have met along the way in creating this book, thank you for sharing your stories and for your generous hospitality.

To my main team Mallory Hughes, always there for me – love you, Tom Allnutt, and Milo Steelfox for the best help ever, I could not function without you and all the smiley faces on my packages.

To Annabel Bate, my sounding board and confidant on all things interiors and design.

To Anna Stanley, so thankful our daddies brought us together.

To Hannah Field, a constant ray of sunshine in my life with unwavering belief in me, especially when I have a wobble.

To Sarah Rowntree, still mainly for fizz, x.

To Shona Gold, my shiny, happy friend.

To Vanessa Quick, my wonderful travel partner.

To Natalie O'Brien, for so much love, always, and laughs.

To Benedict Foley, always there to chew the cud and frame my paintings so beautifully.

To Fabrice Bana, Becs Lyon, Penny Sheehan and Anna Spiro, for sharing some wonderful places with me.

To all the @roomportraitclub members, for the creativity and joy you bring me every day.

To Kit Kemp, for continuing to support and inspire me every step of the way – I'm blown away by your kindness.

To Jenny Mathieson, for everything – your unwavering support and loveliness.

To Martina Mondadori, for your generosity, inspiration and encouragement, it means the world.

To my tribes 'Besties', 'Chartridge Gorgeousness', 'Home Front', 'Delicious Crew', and especially the 'WI' (Nats, Annabel, Geen, Ems and Mireille) – without you all, I don't know where I would be.

To my bestie, Louise Ah-Sun, for ALWAYS being there even for the ridiculous stuff.

To my wonderful family, for all your encouragement and support.

To my super-talented Mama, for everything.

To James, Freds and Marv for your ceaseless love and support. And ever faithful Bon Bon, too. X.